FROM FOAL TO CHAMPION

PHOTOGRAPHS BY DELL HANCOCK

TEXT BY EDWARD L. BOWEN

STEWART, TABORI & CHANG

NEW YORK

Published in 1991 by
Stewart, Tabori & Chang, Inc.
575 Broadway, New York, New York 10012

LIBRARY OF CONGRESS CATALOGING-IN-PUBLICATION DATA

Hancock, Dell.
From foal to champion : raising racehorses in bluegrass Kentucky /
photographs by Dell Hancock ; text by Edward L. Bowen.
p.   cm.
Includes index.
ISBN 1-55670-205-1 : $60.00
1. Race horses—Kentucky.   2. Race horses—Kentucky—Pictorial
works.   3. Thoroughbred horse—Kentucky.   4. Thoroughbred horse—
—Kentucky—Pictorial works.   5. Horse-racing.   6. Horse-racing—
—Pictorial works.   I. Bowen, Edward L.   II. Title.
SF338.H35   1991   90-48334
798.4′0022′2—dc20   CIP

Distributed in the U.S. by Workman Publishing,
708 Broadway, New York, New York 10003
Distributed in Canada by Canadian Manda Group
P.O. Box 920 Station U, Toronto, Ontario M8Z 5P9
Distributed in all other territories by Little,
Brown and Company, International Division, 34 Beacon Street,
Boston, Massachusetts 02108

Printed in Japan

10 9 8 7 6 5 4 3 2 1

To Dad for my love of horses,
and to Mama for my appreciation of art.

CONTENTS

VIGNETTES OF THE TURF

Edward L. Bowen

Chewing gum eventually will come apart in your mouth, transforming into an odd alchemy able to be both powdery and sticky at the same time. I discovered this one morning the summer I was nineteen. I must have circled the barn with Zami Girl twenty times, and she was the fourth or fifth horse I had walked that morning. Chewing gum was all I allotted myself for breakfast, because the real bargain meal at the Monmouth Park kitchen was lunch. For a buck thirty-four you could gorge, and it was not half bad.

The whole idea of heading to the backstretch of a major Thoroughbred racetrack had seemed as romantic to me as hiking across Europe in ill-smelling clothes would to the youth of the next decade. The spell of Thoroughbred rac-

ing was not just an illusion, I was convinced. The racetrack—its history, its color, and especially the nobility of the horses themselves—would surely be the most glamorous, and glorious, of all existences.

At the bottom of the pecking order of the racetrack workers is the hot walker, whose job it is to lead a sweaty animal around the shedrow of the barn until the trainer—the boss, the drill sergeant, as it were—says to stop, to return the horse to the comforts of his dark, cool stall. Between such athletic gigs, the hot walker might be privileged to muck out the stall, pitching the spoiled straw from the stall and replacing it with fresh, sweet, new bedding. It was at this exalted level that I was working for a summer between semesters at the University of Florida.

Monmouth Park is a large, modern, New Jersey shore-resort racetrack begun in the 1940s by a courtly business man named Amory L. Haskell. Give or take a few niceties here and there, however, the backstretch of one racetrack is very much like that of another. A huddle of barns is arranged in rows, with shedrows beneath the eaves of each and varying distances between barns. Tons and tons of hay and straw are often stashed in the loft above the stalls, and at either end of each barn is a trainer's office and a few cramped living quarters for backstretch workers. The major differences between the top tracks and lesser ones is the quality of the horses, and Monmouth Park was very near the top.

The backstretch is a community unto itself, a gypsy caravan that can accommodate the lowlife, the down-and-out, but also the ambitious young man or woman who loves horses and has the intelligence and determination to turn that love into a career as a groom, exercise rider, trainer, or jockey. Somehow, this ramshackle collection of disparate parts hums along more or less smoothly, hitting one stand for sixty or a hundred days and then breaking down its trappings for a trip to the next city, the next race meeting.

During my first week far from my safe, Florida home, I concluded that the romance of the racetrack was a myth. My only ambition was to collect enough money for a bus ride home and head back. The teenager's mortification in admitting this had been a bum idea would have to be swallowed. I just wanted out.

Then, somehow, it all began to round into something like the summer I had imagined. Amazingly, the old clichés about the bracing scent of horse sweat and straw and liniment were based on fact. A particularly urine-soaked patch of bedding in a stall could prove particularly unpleasant, but, on the whole, the animals in fact have a romance, a fineness, to them.

The mere act of getting to work on time and following instructions soon earned me a promotion. Within weeks, I was a groom. This entitled me to dangle from my Levi's hip pockets a pair of heady status symbols: a hoof pick and a rub rag. No private, first class, ever wore his badge of promotion—from the bottom to next to it—with more pride.

Assigned the grooms' task of "rubbing" three horses, I set about my morning routine with relish. These were not just racehorses; they were the scions of years of selective breeding, the heirs to generations of glory on the race-track. I had read of some of their sires and dams, and through their veins coursed the blood of the ages.

Now, it requires being nineteen and in love with images not to recognize that the same could be said of practically every Thoroughbred in the barn at Monmouth Park, or any other racetrack, for the breed traces back to only three foundation sires. Still, the soft feel of Wallingford's coat when I drew the big, heavy brush across his lean withers and back, the breath from the high head of Sir Carran when he knew he was about to race, the fine tendons down Mark Owen's legs when I rolled on four freshly laundered cloth bandages—each with a pleasing symmetry—these were not just visual delights. They felt good. They even smelled good.

For all their stolid mass, racehorses are creatures of life and breath and pulse. Even standing still they give off a heady aura of grace and kinetic glory.

Thus were reinstated the wonders of the turf, the wonders I had learned from reading Walter Farley's *Black Stallion* books and C. W. Anderson's *The Smashers*, from watching races on television and wondrous old movies like *The Winner's Circle* and *National Velvet*. Once homesickness and fear of working around adults were overcome, I was free to experience the racehorse and horse racing in all their complexities.

Work begins before five o'clock. By the time the groom climbs wearily from his cot, usually one old veteran of particular reliability has made his morning feeding rounds. Perhaps there, in the darkness, he pauses to revisit his own dreams as he scoops the clean white oats into the feed tubs. What furlongs of destiny consigned him to his morning rounds instead of the applause of the winner's circle, the spotlight reserved for trainers and owners? The predictable nickers of his hungry flock may be some reward, for in this presunrise ritual he has with them a communion that owner, trainer, and jockey seldom share.

On their own schedules, grooms assemble, the trainer rolls up—often in a big sedan—and the coffee truck starts its noisy rounds to verify the beginning of a new day. The horses are haltered and tethered with a single chain to a screw eye in the stall. Their bobbing heads slap the chains against the smooth old wood of the stalls as the grooms brush away the accumulated straw dust of the night. The next few hours are hectic. Many tasks must be crammed into the morning, after which the day suddenly gives way to a sleepy leisure, which in turn is interrupted in the afternoon by the race itself.

No matter how many horses he has in his care, the trainer arrives each morning with a schedule in his head for each of them. The groom then carries out the program, or prepares his horses to turn over to one of the exercise riders who has shown up by prearrangement or just happens to be around waiting for work. A horse might merely be walked, if he has raced in the last few days or is coming up to a race. More than likely he will be galloped around the track, a mile, maybe two. Fairly often, too, he will have a work—a breeze. This is a move to enhance his speed and conditioning, the closest he will get to a race in the morning. Sometimes the breeze is augmented by working in company with another horse, but usually it is a work in solitude, a moment in the sun that only a few will watch—his trainer, perhaps his owner, and the professional clockers who lurk silently in the stands, stopwatch in hand.

The groom delivers the horse, brushed to perfection, to the exercise rider, helps saddle the horse and give the rider a leg up, and then returns to the stall to muck out. It is easy to muck out a stall when the horse is gone: Scoop up the manure and dirtied straw with a pitchfork; pile it onto a vast, sewn coupling of burlap bags placed in the stall doorway; then fold the corners together over the discarded material, heave the muck sack onto your back, and waddle over to the muck heap between barns. Next you throw the waste onto the stack, which steams as the morning air meets the natural heat. A huge truck will come along to haul it all off, perhaps to some mushroom farmer who pays a fair price for what you want to throw away.

By the time the horse comes back from his work, the groom is ready. His arsenal is comprised of steaming buckets of soapy water and clear water, a soft sponge, and a sweat scraper—a sacred piece of equipment, which with a deft swipe can fling rivulets of water off the horse's side and onto the ground four feet away.

The return of a racehorse from a work is an impressive sight when seen from the ground. The trainer, seated in a Western saddle aboard a stout lead pony, accompanies the prancing beast, as the exercise rider tries to get the horse to relax the muscles tested in a sprint of perhaps a half-mile, or six furlongs. The horse is a picture of excitement and exertion—eyes wide, sinews prominent from the recent effort, veins standing out on neck and shoulder. Creamy foam escapes around the bit and drops in flecks down on his chest and the ground below. Again, the scents are assailant, a specific pungence duplicated nowhere.

The groom's eyes seek the rider's and the question is mutely asked: How did he do? What do you think? Perhaps a glint in the eye or a smirk will reveal that the

Crisscrossed with shadows, a stable hand rakes the shedrow at Aiken Training Center, South Carolina. The winter quarters of many outstanding runners, Aiken was built in 1941 to serve as a proving ground for top young horses—including the great gelding Kelso and, more recently, the champion Forty Niner—and as a place to freshen up older campaigners.

exercise rider plans to bet on this horse next time out, or maybe he or she will say outright: "You're gonna jog your beat tomorrow, kid," or, "This s.o.b.'s got a heart the size of a pea."

Regardless, the groom's work of the moment is to get the horse unsaddled and bathed, so the cooling out—the forty-five or so minutes of walking—can begin. The animal must not be allowed to cool too quickly, for his muscles might cramp—a condition known as "tying up." He is given one chance to sip from a water bucket, held to him at chest level, and he dives for it lustily; however, he is not allowed to drink much at any one time.

While one groom holds the horse's shank, two others, one on each side, hurry through the bath. Soapy water is sponged on, followed by clear water, the liquid cascading down the bulges of bone and muscle and tendons. Then the remaining clean water is splashed from the bucket up under the horse's flanks to clear away any additional soap and grit. His feet are lifted one by one and cleaned with a hoof pick to remove dirt and stones that might eventually cause him discomfort. He is rubbed nearly dry, blanketed, and turned over to the hot walker.

The hot walker leads the horse over under the shedrow, where they take a position in a line of other horses in similar stages of physical debriefing. Every few laps, the hot walker hollers, "Whoa back!"—a warning to the parade that he is pausing to let his charge take a quick sip from his water bucket. The parade continues, the horse's tautness gradually subsides, and soon hot walker and athlete slide into an easy, daydream-enhanced gait, until the groom's regular checks convince him it is time to stop, to return the combatant to his stall.

When the workload permits, even the grooms and trainers and exercise riders take their turns as hot walkers from one hour to the next. It is a time for dreams. "Maybe this two-year-old to my right is going to be a good one.

A family of swans decorates the grounds of Claiborne Farm. Rarely are horses the only crop
on the farms in the Bluegrass. As well as ducks and swans, cats abound, dogs
serve on watch duty, and herds of cattle are often used to graze the pastures in rotation.
Goats and chickens are ubiquitous as well; the expression "get his goat"
refers to stealing a rival horse's stall mate, as many high-strung racers gain solace from
the company of a goat. The great Man o' War's companion was a game
cock; other horses prefer a hen; still others, a donkey.

Maybe in time he'll be running against the crackerjack colt Woody Stephens has brought down from New York for the Sapling Stakes. Maybe that big, liver chestnut son of the Triple Crown winner up ahead will make it to the winner's circle. Maybe the burly bay colt I walked last week—the one so studdish he tries to mount any living thing, including the hot walker—will settle down and behave like what he is, the son of a Kentucky Derby winner."

By late morning, the hustle-bustle has slowed. Grooms sit on tack boxes, rolling freshly laundered bandages, curling long leather lead shanks into their brass fittings, or raking symmetrical lines into the dampened dirt of the shedrow. There is a sense of order to a shedrow: the pleasant scent of the shedrow dirt, the sounds of horses eating oats, the scrape of the rake. The hours, so quick to pass in early morning, grow long and heavy. Next will be the stroll to the kitchen, the midday nap, and, on some days, the call to the post.

The Bold Reasoning colt could be any kind," Sally Hill heard her husband say one morning when he came back to their rented house from the track at Saratoga. She was not yet clued in to all the clichés of the turf, so she was not so sure what he meant. Still, Jim Hill delivered this bit of horse talk with such emphasis that it seemed it *had* to be exciting.

No horseman can bring himself to say a young colt or filly is *great*—not until they have shown the magical speed and admirable courage to run past their rivals into the record books. Thus, *could be any kind* is a safe way of praising, or putting dreams to words. It gives the seer an out: "I'm not saying he *will* be great, but what I am saying is the way he worked this morning, he could be, well, *any kind*." How else would you say it?

The son of Bold Reasoning, the two-year-old in question, on that morning in 1976 was about to launch the young veterinarian and his wife onto one of those voyages of life that come only to the few, and then by as much a whim of the muses as by intellect and work. The colt had been purchased by the Hills in partnership with another young couple, Mickey and Karen Taylor, at a yearling sale in Kentucky the year before. The cost was $17,500.

Now, you take two young couples who like each other, who go to the movies on weekends and the guys talk sports and the girls talk babies and clothes, and you would find that $17,500 would be a lot to come up with for the four of them. In the world of Kentucky yearling sales, however, seventeen-five for a colt is a bargain. This is a high-stakes game starring sheikhs from Arabia, moguls from industry, sportsmen from yore. The Hills and the Taylors could not have guessed that ultimately a yearling half brother to "the Bold Reasoning colt" would command a price of $13.1 million.

Mickey and Karen Taylor were from the town of White Swan, Washington, but they named the Bold Reasoning colt after a more prominent town in their state. Thus, the name of Seattle Slew was affixed to the dark, husky, willful colt that the keen eye of veterinarian Hill had perceived as a yearling might be something more than just another horse.

More than a year later, the colt was approaching racing fitness under Hill and his trainer, a young horseman named Billy Turner. In the fall, at Belmont Park, the racing world was impressed as Slew zipped unbeaten through three races, including the Champagne Stakes—the climactic event for two-year-olds at the time.

Each discipline has its ultimate goal, the composite of target and dream that makes the centerpiece. In politics, it is the White House; in movies, the Oscars; in baseball, the World Series. In horse racing, the ultimate is a complicated arrangement known as the Triple Crown. This series of races for three-year-olds kicks off with the Kentucky Derby. Through all the winter and early spring, the Kentucky Derby looms as the single most important event on the American turf, and yet, as soon as a horse has won it—has stood in the winner's circle in a garland of roses—he is seen merely to have made the first stride. Two weeks later, he must face the Preakness Stakes in Maryland, and then, in another three weeks, the Belmont Stakes in New York. Together the three races form the Triple Crown—an oft-questioned arrangement whose schedule can be criticized as too demanding. Yet, in the final analysis, it is a song of perfection, for the horse who can win all three races is a rare and admirable animal—one whose very being justifies all the sweat, money, and emotions poured into the sport of Thoroughbred racing.

Being built, by and large, upon English tenets, it is not surprising that the American colonies from early days imitated the sporting patterns of England. In the seventeenth century, Thoroughbred racing developed almost concurrently on the two sides of the Atlantic, but it was England that was the wellspring for the breed itself.

One step farther back into the mist, one finds the inevitable parallel of warfare and sport. The development of the light-boned, refined, speedy horse known today as the Thoroughbred racehorse came in part from a need for a better weapon in the blood stakes of the battlefield.

The age of the knight in armor required huge, massive animals capable of carrying the heavy equipage that the warfare of the day entailed. Then the technology of warfare changed as English archers in leather jerkins came into prominence at Agincourt, Crecy, and Poitiers. The advent of gunpowder came next.

The concepts of cavalry proved adaptable. The development of horses light enough to be quick and agile and still strong enough to stand up to the demands of strenuous campaigns allowed horses to remain pivotal to warfare midway into the twentieth century. Along the way, man

A band of yearlings at a creek in a field during a snowstorm. Yearlings are turned out in
every kind of weather except that which brings an icy snow, which
could be damaging to their young, unshod feet.

also developed his most noble partner in sport—the Thoroughbred.

The breed evolved from the importation of Eastern horses; as early as the Crusades the so-called desert horse had been admired by the European adventurers. Exported to be crossed with heavier mares from England's existing stock, these Arab, Barb, and Turk stallions set the path to the modern breed. As early as the reign of Henry VIII, there was a royal stud in England, and it was not long thereafter that the racing of horses at Newmarket and elsewhere became one of the favorite royal pastimes. "The Sport of Kings" was out of the womb.

Over several centuries, racing—and the tracing of bloodlines—was formalized, so that today the *General Stud Book* of England and its counterparts in the United States and many other countries trace the bloodlines of all existing Thoroughbreds. By common consent of all racing states in this country, for example, no horse can participate in a pari-mutuel Thoroughbred race (one in which betting is allowed) unless its lineage is certified by The Jockey Club—and this certification requires the horse's ancestry being traceable for eight generations in the *General Stud Book.*

Central to the goals of the Thoroughbred breeder in the founding land is the Epsom Derby, also known as the English Derby or, to acknowledge its sponsor, the Ever Ready Derby. This event was inaugurated in 1780 and for over two centuries has enjoyed status virtually akin to a national holiday in England. As the Empire lapped upon the shores of many lands only to recede, the Derby has held firm as a bastion of an arrogant history and a noble present. It is well styled as The Blue Ribband of the Turf.

While the Derby has no equal in the minds of Great Britain's general public, it is linked among those involved with the sport with two other events—the Two Thousand Guineas and the St. Leger. Over the years these three tests earned the status of being the most important races for three-year-olds, and they eventually became known as the Triple Crown. Quick to borrow this concept, several race circuits in the United States attempted to carve out similar status for three races of their own. New York, for example, tried with the Withers Stakes, Belmont Stakes, and the Realization. This series more or less imitated the English pattern, which begins in midspring with the 1-mile Guineas, continues in June with the 1½-mile Epsom Derby, and concludes much later, in September, with the 1¾-mile St. Leger

Creating a sporting event that the public embraces is not so much a matter of logical planning as happenstance, however. None of the designed Triple Crown imitators ever caught on. Instead, in this country a series of races exists—all in a hurry to be run—that moved to the top on

their own, without mere humans orchestrating their connection. These are the Derby—that Americana rose event that speaks to the Mark Twain in our national heritage as well as to our English roots—the Preakness, a fried-chicken-and-crabcake nostalgia trip near the Chesapeake Bay; and the Belmont Stakes in the vast elegance of Belmont Park on Long Island. All these races were overseen by different impresarios; none was purposely coordinated; and yet by the 1930s they had become linked as the American Triple Crown. So quickly does one race follow the other that this Triple Crown grips the public more than any other horse racing event—more, to be truthful, even, than the original Triple Crown interests English sportsmen and punters.

At the time Seattle Slew was being readied for his bid for Triple Crown history, the sweep had been accomplished by nine horses before him, eight of which had raced before 1950. Sir Barton had come first in 1919, to be followed by Gallant Fox (1930), Omaha (1935), War Admiral (1937), Whirlaway (1941), Count Fleet (1943), Assault (1946), and Citation (1948). After Citation there was a drought of Triple Crown winners. Just as it had seemed a year was a poor one when there was no Triple Crown winner, it began to seem as if there never would be another.

Marvelous young princes came to the line in their attempt at the ultimate tiara of racing. Native Dancer, Nashua, Majestic Prince, Northern Dancer, and Canonero II were among the champions who won two legs of the spring voyage to destiny, but somehow saw the sweep elude them. Eventually, a quarter-century would pass before the three races fell to the same horse. When that champion of champions came along, it seemed right that he should be a truly heroic animal. Thus, nothing could have been more fitting than that the horse to break through after all those years was an animal who seemed larger than life. A bright chestnut colt with impeccable breeding, his name was Secretariat.

Nothing explains the arrival of a great racehorse like Secretariat, any more than a Churchill, a Babe Ruth, a Picasso, an Olivier can truly have been anticipated. When a great horse comes along, a horse of boundless fire and pride and sheer capacity for speed and distance, he is a creation not to be questioned, but to be savored.

Secretariat captured America as he captured the Triple Crown—the Derby with finesse, the Preakness with authority, and, finally, the Belmont by thirty-one lengths. To watch the replay after all those years of the Belmont is to feel again a moment of dramatic and artistic perfection. Secretariat ran that day "like a tremendous machine," intoned the amazed announcer, Chick Anderson. But looking back, one sees Secretariat not as a machine, but as an allegory of myth.

Lured by the scent of breakfast bacon sizzling on the grill, a Jack Russell terrier waits
hopefully outside the backstretch kitchen at Saratoga.

It was four years after Secretariat's Triple Crown sweep that Seattle Slew made his own bid for immortality. He had the opportunity to add one historic fillip to the history of the classics. No horse ever had been undefeated at the time he had completed the Triple Crown—not Citation, not even Secretariat.

The appealing young owners, styled "the Slew Crew," and the articulate trainer, Billy Turner, tuned this fine instrument of a horse to perfection. He came into his three-year-old campaign unbeaten, and unbeaten he faced the Triple Crown. When it was over, he had in fact won all three races with his lusty yearning for speed. He was that most unexpected of phenomena—an unbeaten winner of the American Triple Crown.

The dramas of track and human relationships that followed underscored the whims of fate. Seattle Slew lost in his first race after the Belmont; his owners parted company with his trainer; he got sick and nearly died; he lost again after a comeback; and his regular rider was replaced. Having squirmed enough upon the rack of reality, however, the Slew Crew soon was handed again a series of sublime moments.

By the fall of Seattle Slew's four-year-old season, he had been surpassed in many a racing fan's heart by the gritty Affirmed, who had won the 1978 Triple Crown in an excruciating series of battles with another fabulous colt, Alydar. When Seattle Slew and Affirmed were brought out for the Marlboro Cup, it marked a first in racing history: the very first meeting of two Triple Crown winners on the racetrack. Seattle Slew, the darling of 1977, was now somehow seen as the villain on Marlboro Day. As the sedate, professional Affirmed was paraded in the paddock, Slew was actually booed as he pranced into his prerace sweat.

Once the gates opened, though, it was Slew who owned the day. It was a race in which the tactic was of the utmost

The stallion graveyard is a tradition on many of Kentucky's oldest horse farms. In honor of
their champions, owners often bury at least the head and heart of the
deceased. Claiborne's rough-hewn stones mark the graves of some of the breed's most
influential sires, including the imported stallions Blenheim II and Sir
Gallahad III, the powerful Bold Ruler and his brilliant heir Secretariat, Princequillo,
Round Table, and the 1984 Kentucky Derby winner Swale.

simplicity, namely, to outrun all the others from the beginning. This strategy was perfect for Slew. He led from the gate, he led at halfway through, and he led at the end.

Seattle Slew, the $17,500 yearling, won fourteen of his seventeen races in three years and earned $1,208,726 for the Taylors and Hills. What makes him an even more remarkable bargain, however, has been his lasting and profound influence on the breed. His owners have had brilliant success managing his career as a stallion. He has sired such horses as Slew o' Gold, a champion of sculpted physical presence, and a literal "slew" of other successful runners. Another of his sons was Swale, who won for the historic Claiborne Farm its long-sought goal—the Kentucky Derby.

Seattle Slew, once the warrior of wide eye and a boundless love of speed, is now a stout, complacent stallion standing at Three Chimneys Farm in Kentucky. He was, and is, a horse that went even beyond dreams.

While it is patently obvious that the female parent is as important as the male to the genetic makeup of the foal, testicles dominate the development of the Thoroughbred breed. The disparate numbers that nature decreed the two sexes can produce make the male horse the more expensive, the more prolific, the more honored.

Given a gestation period of about eleven months, a mare is lucky if in her lifetime she produces ten foals that get to the races. Contrast that to a great stallion, who might be sent books for some fifty mares annually for fifteen years. The great stallion Northern Dancer, for example, has sired more than six hundred foals.

These disparate numbers etch the importance of sires and male lines into the consciousness of breeders. The realization that, in any given mating selection, the mare and stallion each account for 50 percent of the genetic menu is engulfed by the sheer volume of productivity that the sire possesses. Sire lines become the most commonly referenced link to the past, and breeding patterns seek to utilize the popular sire lines far more frequently than tenuous female families. Thus, Northern Dancer and his sons—potentates such as Nureyev, Lyphard, and Nijinsky II—become the focus of genetic dynasties.

In the boom years of the 1980s, prices for stallion service grew to such heights than an individual stallion could be valued at as much as $40 million. Typically, a stallion's ownership is divided into forty shares. The owner of each share is entitled to send one mare to the stallion each year, and the extra stud services that the stallion might perform create additional income or opportunities for the shareholders. When yearling prices skyrocketed, the cost of breeding to a stallion who might father such a yearling went through the roof as well. Although the rapid rise finally abated, the cost of breeding to the best stallions today remains well up into six figures.

Being potential gold mines, stallions are treated like pampered kings. The accoutrements of the stallion barn often reflect a subconsciously masculine identification with the horses themselves. Stallion barns are likely to be decorated with masculine-oriented decorations, such as fighting cocks or hounds, while the brass door fittings and shiny halter plates underscore that the animals within are to be treated regally.

While copulation is a mysterious force of power and life, many of the variables of the equine mating process are taken out of the procedure. For the sake of the stallion's well-being, the mare is bathed and then teased by a non-breeding male of indestructible libido to ascertain that she is in season and thus unlikely to kick out when the stallion attempts to mount her. Her estrous cycle is carefully monitored, and the stallion is used at the optimum time for conception. As a final safety measure, the mare is hobbled, or one of her legs is held up, so she does not have the balance to kick the stallion in the vulnerability of his mating ritual.

The stallion is led to the bathed and tested mare, erupts into a sexually obsessed beast seemingly unnoticing of anything but this one urge, and then quickly recedes to the placidity of one whose every need has been attended. Often, the schedule of the breeding season dictates two such sessions per day in the breeding shed. Still, for all the seeming attempt to make the process devoid of nature, there is a raw beauty to the sight of a stallion—neck arched, nostrils flared, prance exaggerated—as he approaches the breeding shed with the knowledge through habit and association that yet another mate is awaiting.

Having been bred, the female of the species from that time on receives a special attention of her own. As life is confirmed, and flourishes, within her, she, too, is treated as a being of profoundly special status. As foaling time nears, she will be watched over carefully, her condition monitored by day crews and night watchmen. Finally, she will be taken into a spacious, deeply bedded stall, where attendants will do all they can to reduce the hazards that attend the birth of so large a creature. Afterward, perhaps the following morning, the new mother and her scrawny foal will be introduced to the outdoors in their individual paddock. Eventually, they will join other mares and their foals in green rolling fields. The youngster stretches his limbs, breathes in the air of spring. He was bred and will be trained for the purposes of man, but man does not seek ultimately to conquer him.

As a budding athlete, he will be trained to recognize that the smaller species is his master and the metal bit that will guide him through his competitive life is not of his own forging. Still, there is a freedom he saves for himself— the freedom of speed, in answer to the private call of a pulse that runs untamed through bone, and blood, and sinew.

Already back in foal, these seven broodmares graze in the October frost shortly after their
foals have been weaned. The separation of weanlings from their dams on the first
Tuesday in October leaves some of the younger broodmares calling out for their brood
throughout the first night. If a mare has had an uncomplicated, easy delivery she
may be bred on the ninth day after birth—called the "foal heat," when she is receptive to
a stallion for a short time. Any questions about her condition and the vet will
postpone the session, pending a clean bill of health.

A big, husky son of Northern Dancer entered the ring. He was larger and longer than his sire. In fact, he looked more like his lanky dark grandsire, Nearctic, than his chunky, little blaze-faced sire, Northern Dancer—the Canadian colt who had won the 1964 Kentucky Derby.

The Northern Dancer colt was the star of the 1968 Woodbine Canadian-bred yearling sale in Toronto. That evening, he was purchased for $84,000, a figure that moved Woodbine into the big leagues. The colt was in the consignment of Canada's premier horseman, E. P. Taylor, master of Windfields Farm. Taylor for years had sold his yearlings in a way one can sell only to a captive audience. Amid a congenial ambience of hospitality and semi-high stakes at his pleasant farm in Oshawa, Ontario, he would offer to invited guests the members of his yearling crop. Each had a price. You took it, or you took a drink and awaited the next lot. Once half of the crop was sold, the sale was over. Saunter up the bar, me lads; there'll be no more horses sold today. Taylor happily took the remainder to place into his racing stable, and then invariably wound up competing with the new purchases of his friends and clients.

The most famous moment at a Windfields sale had occurred in 1962, when a smallish son of Nearctic-Natalma had been offered for $25,000. At that time and place, the figure was high stakes, indeed, and the suspicion has lingered through the years—eventually anointed with the patina of factual lore—that the management at Windfields had purposely priced the colt out of the market. The colt, later to be named Northern Dancer, was, in fact, passed over at $25,000, but a substantial list of horsemen today claim to have been there and almost purchased him.

Racing in Taylor's turquoise silks with golden polka dots, Northern Dancer became the first Canadian to win an American classic. He followed his Kentucky Derby

The ironwork of the fine old Saratoga grandstand evokes nostalgia in many a racegoer. Spanning twenty-four
days—a short but telling season—the Saratoga meet includes four graded
stakes held on consecutive Saturdays: the Whitney; the Alabama for three-year-old fillies;
the Travers (also known as the Midsummer Derby) for three-year-olds;
and the Hopeful, so-called because its contestants, all two-year-old colts, are
too young to raise any guarantees, just hopes.

triumph with a win in the Preakness, but ran third in the Belmont to miss the Triple Crown. Returning to his homeland, he won Canada's most historic and colorful race, the Queen's Plate, and soon thereafter was retired to his owner's farm. He had proven that Ontario in general, and Taylor specifically, could produce a world-class horse.

In 1968, Taylor abandoned his private, prepriced sale to support the local auction. The big bay colt who topped the bidding was purchased by a representative for the financier Charles W. Engelhard. An American, Engelhard was known to the world of finance for his exploits in South Africa, where he forged an astonishingly lucrative career in such commodities as gold and platinum. He took good-naturedly the mirthful rumor that he was the model for Ian Fleming's character Goldfinger in the James Bond thriller of the same name.

To many travelers of the world, England is the epitome of the turf. Although he had flourishing stables in both South Africa and the United States, Engelhard set his sights keenly on the great prizes of Europe. Thus, the Northern Dancer–Flaming Page colt who had commanded a record price on a Toronto evening in 1968 was sent abroad. Engelhard's key trainer was Vincent O'Brien, who had won the Epsom Derby with Sir Ivor for Raymond Guest earlier that year. O'Brien's hillocky training grounds, located near Dublin, in Cashel, was where the colt was sent to prepare for history.

No purchase of a horse can be said to be a certainty before the fact, but the acquisition of the Northern Dancer colt was more than a little oblique. In fact, Engelhard had sent O'Brien to Ontario not to look for sons of the little Northern Dancer—whose stamina was far from ascertained in the European context—but to look at a son of Ribot. *There* was a horse to sire European runners. Ribot was a wonder horse: English-foaled, but based in Italy, he had been the unbeaten star of Europe in 1955 and 1956.

Sixteen times he had been under starter's orders, and sixteen times he had been led into the winner's enclosure.

Great prizes of England and France, as well as Italy, fell to Ribot. He was so valuable that after standing initially in Europe he was acquired on a lease by John W. Galbreath to come to stand at Darby Dan Farm in Kentucky. In an era when purchasing an entire horse for $1 million still was a headline event, Galbreath shelled out $1.35 million merely to lease Ribot for five years. By 1968, Ribot had ascended to the top of international sires, and Engelhard himself had won classics in England and Ireland with Ribot's sons. Yet O'Brien, on his visit to Windfields, had not been so impressed with the Ribot colt from the champion mare Canadiana. Instead his gaze was drawn again and again to the big bay by Northern Dancer. He stood over a lot of ground; he had a certain look.

O'Brien wanted him at Cashel, wanted to see just what manner of beast he could help this horse become. Engelhard chose for the colt a classic name redolent of grace and airiness. The colt was named Nijinsky II. The great ballet dancer's widow followed his career with bemused interest. In 1969 he won all five of his races and was regarded as England's champion two-year-old. The campaign of 1970, when Nijinsky was three, would tell the tale.

Epsom Downs, where the most historic race in the world has been run since 1780, is a common. Racecourse organizers might have preferred that dogs and children not dance beside the railing where the inward camber of the ground gives way to a testing uphill run to the finishing post, but there was not a great deal they could do about the public's right to be there. Even more so than the Kentucky Derby, the Epsom Derby is a combination holiday and sporting event for both the upper crust and the hoi polloi. If the sum of all things English needed circumscription into a single venue, Derby Day at Epsom would be the most effective vehicle.

The Queen of England and untold hundreds of thousands of her subjects watched, or strained to see, as the greatest rider of his day, Lester Piggott, tantalized them into thinking that the unbeaten Nijinsky was in trouble.

The flashiest horse in the field was Gyr, the big son of the great Sea-Bird. Gyr was a colt of such compelling potential that his trainer had postponed his own retirement just to see the colt through his three-year-old campaign. Halfway between Tattenham Corner and the finishing post, Gyr looked invincible, and Nijinsky seemed to be nowhere. The colt of "foreign" bloodlines, with their whispered stamina limits, was in a pinch. Then Piggott asked him to run. Within a few strides, the picture changed.

Nijinsky of Canada dashed to the fore, running clear, running free. The Derby was over, the Derby was his.

Sir Gaylord, two-year-old champion of 1961, half-brother to Secretariat, and one of the world's most prominent stallions, looked across the neck-high top rail of his paddock with some bemusement. At his feet was an unusual sight. Stallions by nature fight each other, so their paddocks are separated by wide lanes; and yet here was another of his own kind sort of rolled up at his feet.

The animal who had interrupted Sir Gaylord's placid morning was the stallion Forli. An undefeated champion in Argentina, he had been imported to the United States by A. B. Hancock, Jr., owner of Claiborne Farm. Forli briefly had continued his unbeaten racing career in this country until a leg injury had forced his retirement. Seventy-five days of confinement to his stall followed.

A. B. Hancock was a large man whose intimidating air was aided and abetted by a resounding voice. He had earned the nickname of "Bull" as a youngster, and the name seemed to have shaped his image ever since. That morning at Claiborne when Forli was to be turned out, though, Bull Hancock had a helpless, sinking feeling.

Claiborne House, part of Claiborne's vast operation encompassing 3,375 acres divided into five farms:
the 644-acre Raceland center for the yearlings; the main farms, Claiborne and
Marchmont, covering 1,974 acres; the 414-acre Clay Farm; the 261-acre
Cherry Valley; and an 82-acre parcel known as the Annex, located down the road.

The dignified Marchmont House (top), is a stately example of the Victorian
mansions built to overlook the rolling hills of their owner's
farms. Xalapa (bottom), one of the most beautiful and historic farms in the Bluegrass
region, was settled in 1827. It is known for its mortarless stone walls
and the venerable sycamores and chestnut trees that grace the landscape.

Fayette County, Kentucky is endowed with a great concentration of horse farms, their acreage
sweeping a rangy arc to the north of Lexington. Normandy Farm (top), received
its name from the style used by Philadelphia architect Horace Trumbauer to build
its foaling barn. Middlebrook Farm (bottom), was built around 1835 and
enjoyed a sterling reputation as one of Kentucky's eight antebellum private boarding schools.

Any horseman knows that a horse confined for so long is likely to be a hazard to itself when it is first released. Hancock was born to the horse business and to Claiborne, and he knew the proper precautions: Place men along the fencerow and in the corners to wave off any attempt at real speed that might put Forli in a precarious position. Bull himself was in the center of the paddock when the young stallion prospect was turned loose.

Forli sensed his freedom, took a few cautious steps, and then sought out an unguarded spot in the fenceline. Thereupon he attempted a leap to freedom, but his will was stronger than his limbs and he settled to earth at the feet of Sir Gaylord. It was a heart-freezing moment. Were all the efforts and professionalism expended in saving this horse to be undone in a moment? Had the nature of the animal outwitted the intelligence of man once again?

Happily, Forli scrambled to his feet unhurt. He quickly recovered, and he went on to have a long and successful stallion career at Claiborne, his most notable son being Forego, a four-time Horse of the Year.

Some years later, in 1970, Forli was connected to another moment of helpless frustration for Bull Hancock. Hancock had bred Forli to a mare named Continue, hoping for a foal who might bring something he had ever yearned for, but never attained: victory in the Kentucky Derby. Now, from 1915 until 1970, only one filly had won the Derby, so a breeder's Derby hopes for any particular mating were considered more or less sunk whenever a filly was born. The night the Forli–Continue foal was born, the nightman had double bad news for Hancock, and it sent him into a rage of audible passion, punctuated with a nicely executed kick of a water bucket. Not only was the foal a filly, but it had been born with only one eye.

Flash forward two years, to 1972, and the one-eyed filly, named Tuerta, comes home first in the Blue Hen Stakes at Delaware Park. By autumn, Hancock, master breeder, world-renowned horseman, is felled by cancer. Many of Claiborne's horses are sold that fall, but Hancock's widow and four children decide to keep Tuerta. This is in part due to judgment—some of the fillies have to be kept as future broodmares—but also due to sentiment: The filly whose entry into the world had caused such dismay in the heart of Bull Hancock had been the last horse he ever saw carry his colors to victory in a stakes race. Tuerta, the one-eyed filly that should have been a colt, was sent home to the nurturing acreage of her birth.

In 1981, Tuerta produced a dark colt sired by Seattle Slew. On seeing him, Mrs. Hancock immediately had one of those inexplicable feelings that horses sometimes give you; more often than not these are dreams disguised as intuition, but in this case she was correct. The Seattle Slew–Tuerta colt *was* special.

In 1982, Claiborne and its longtime partner, William Haggin Perry, sold interests in their yearling crop to others in a package known as the Raceland partnership. The deal involved the various members of the partnership picking yearlings in turn. Mrs. Hancock drew fifth, and Seth Hancock chose the Tuerta colt to race in the farm's historic orange colors.

Recalling the colt's tendency to flop down, go to sleep, and snore loudly, some on the farm suggested Foghorn as a name. Mrs. Hancock sought something more respectful, a name in keeping with her late husband's long-harbored preference for one-syllable names. Thus, the colt from the one-eyed mare was called Swale.

Flash forward again, to 1984. It was a spring day in Kentucky, Derby Day, the day of days to Hancocks and folk of their ilk. Never had the Claiborne silks crossed the finish first with the roses on the line—until that day. Swale—little Foghorn of the yearlings paddocks—rolled home all alone. *Weep no more my lady.* Claiborne Farm has won the Derby.

Epilogue: What a tug-of-war the gods of the turf had with Swale. After the heady moments in the winner's circle on Derby Day, a swirl of fortunes followed—Preakness Day, unplaced in the second classic; Belmont Day, a return to glory, a galloping winner; eight days later, sudden death, the cause never discovered.

No matter how much talent an athlete possesses, success depends on training and conditioning. Out of shape or unsophisticated in their crafts, Jim Brown and O. J. Simpson would have been cut down at the line, Michael Jordan would be earthbound and confused, Steffi Graf a wasted prodigy. So it is with the racehorse. For all the sense of power a true champion might exude in the stretch, the horse is an animal that has to be brought along, a talent that must be carefully managed. The urge to flee is natural in the horse, and compatible with man's purposes, but it is a harmony that must be developed.

From the time most foals are born, they are handled daily. Tiny halters are slipped over their heads when they are so small that the headgear tends to fall sloppily onto their necks. When the mares are taken in their daily routines from field to barn and back, the young foal gets used to being "led" by a handler. He is merely going the way his instinct calls for him to go—with the safety of his mother's bulk and scent—but eventually this natural urge becomes a learned discipline. With the confidence born of months on earth, he will challenge the idea of being led, like a teenager flexing his vague sense of independence, but eventually he will again succumb.

At regular intervals come veterinarians, with all manner of implements, pressing touches, and strange smells. The foal is wormed, inoculated, examined from head to tail. Then, too, the farrier comes with rasp and file—often enough that, soon, standing with each foot in turn held up seems virtually natural. Sometimes, in such visits by the

It's been said that half of racing is a waiting game: waiting for a filly to finally show the
promise she surely has, waiting for the big horse to be ready for a major
race. Time passes more easily with the *The Racing Form*, a cup of coffee, or a game of
cards. Here, Warner Jones, chairman of the board at Churchill Downs,
plays a hand with trainer Steve Penrod, observed by assistant trainer Paul McGee.

blacksmith for filing his young hooves, the foal can nestle against his holder so solidly that an extra nap can be slipped in during the once-unsettling process.

By the time a foal is weaned—taken from its mother's side—its levels of maturity and curiosity are such that the trauma passes quickly. There are frightening moments, to be sure. The old familiar comfort is gone, the one constancy in a world of sights and smells and expressive nickers. Still, a lot of friends have been led over to the same field, and the youngsters begin to enjoy the fun of competition—their first races. In the roughhousing of weanling days come hints of what is to come. Battle-back-or-be-subdued is a lesson that the owners of a field of foals cannot dictate, but therein begin some early sparring sessions not without relationship to the race track.

The heat of weaning time gives way to a bracing chill, a changing landscape of colors, and then those snowy mornings that are soft and stinging at the same time. January 1 comes and a weanling is officially a yearling. The winter lingers, but then the first signs of springtime arrive.

By now, a Thoroughbred yearling might be superficially scarred from the mock combat of young creatures learning their nature. He seems to have become thoroughly indoctrinated in the roles that man chooses to play, and yet his world is still embryonic. On farms where the aim is to prepare a crop of sale animals, the routine might change during the spring. For the fashionable July and August sales at Keeneland and Saratoga, the clientele expects a product that is not quite baby, but not racehorse, either.

The farm routine changes for such animals. A sales yearling is taken into his dark, cool stall for longer hours, his exercise is likely to be prescribed rather than free-form, and the time he spends being curried and pampered is extended. By middle July, his coat glints in the sunlight—a masterpiece of apparent potential.

A foal's curiosity extends to his dam, who waits patiently as he sniffs answers to his
own mysterious questions. Still only weeks old, he is yet
unnamed, and is identified only through the name of his dam.

Sale week is not necessarily the most comforting time for a young horse. If possessed of a pedigree fraught with quality, if correctly conformed and sound, if intelligent and alert, he might be such an appealing prospect that he is brought out many times from his temporary stall/home at the sale grounds. Walk this way, walk that. Stand still. Let a stranger run a hand down the legs, now walk away. Stand again. Then back to the stall. How many times? For what purpose?

Then, after that routine is mastered, the handler suddenly leads the colt or filly in the other direction. After one more spate of inspections, he is heading away from the stall into a small dirt ring. Loud voices, a raucous chant, a strange hammer sound, odd lights, and an unbelievable collection of people.

The rapid chant of the auctioneer might mean nothing to the young colt or filly, but it has a sorcerer's power over consignor and bidder. How many figures does this one demand? Is it $1,100 at tops—as for the champion gelding John Henry and hundreds of thousands of the forever nondescript? Or, perhaps, this is a son of a Triple Crown winner, or another Northern Dancer, a first foal from the filly champion, an animal blessed with the "black type" with which stakes victories are listed in the formatted catalog. Some of these command princely fortunes, untried athletes sold literally for millions of dollars.

Whatever the yearling's sale status, a change in routine is forthcoming. After being sold, he or she is likely to be loaded by unfamiliar personnel onto a vehicle crowded with strange horses, transported to another farm, and led to a new stall. Days with the dam are long forgotten and soon, too, must be forgotten the carefree days of frolic among old friends.

In due time, the Thoroughbred yearling—now approaching two years old—begins lessons different from anything in the past, but somehow related. Not just led anymore with a halter and shank, but with a strange metal bit; then a weight is put on his or her withers. A few days later, there is the awkward feeling of something towering above. A rider is up.

At farms and training centers across America, the crop of nearly 50,000 foals-turned-yearlings begin to edge closer to the status of young racehorses. They are ridden carefully in single file under shed rows; jogged and then galloped in fields or on tracks; made to do figure-eights to become used to being reined left and right; and asked to take turns being in front of, behind, and between other yearlings.

Then come gallops, always under a tight rein— sometimes with expert riders who help instinctively the athletic use of a young horse's limbs, sometimes with awkward, unskilled horsemen who fight against the bit and, in a stunningly short time, can instill bad habits that forever will work against the horse's chance to be a successful competitor. At length, those headlong gallops into the sun of weanling days seem about to be repeated.

Finally, they ask the horse not just to gallop along with other horses, but to run.

For all the impatience a young horse might feel, for the rider and trainer to remain patient is paramount. A workout that puts too much stress on the fledgling athlete might instill a speed-craziness in him that lingers long into his racing days, when harnessing of speed for the final furlongs is essential to efficient performance. Worse, too much too soon for the yearling might simply bring a level of fatigue, confusion, and physical misuse that renders the youngster but a shadow of the potential inherent in his genes. Months go by. Daily gallops grow longer, interspersed with exhilarating speed works known as breezes. Never quite out of control, but drinking the wind in delicious gulps, the approaching two-year-old gradually sheds the aura of the youngster and grows toward the racehorse.

Come January 1, he is not yet ready to run, but the months grow short. Soon, he will be sent away on another voyage. Again, there are strange new surroundings, a strange trainer, a strange groom—the hustle-bustle of the racetrack. The young horse does not know what awaits, but the atmosphere of excitement, of constantly coiled energy, is consistent now with more and more serious training.

He is likely to have setbacks. A leg irritation known as bucked shins will interrupt most two-year-olds' training for six weeks or so at a time. Or, perhaps, owner and trainer will simply conclude that the horse's young, gawky limbs need more time to develop to enable the colt to face the early-maturing bullies already beginning to crowd into *Racing Form* headlines. Like all adolescents, these equine athletes develop on different life rhythms.

Finally, though, a strange feeling begins to pervade the latest "natural" routine in a lifetime of changing patterns.

Feed is taken away at a strange time in the day; grooming is at an unusual hour. They take the horse out of the stall in the heat of afternoon, take him to his first race. He is surrounded by crowds of people, unfamiliar horses, jockeys in bright shirts. He is led by a pony to the post. He enters the starting gate.

When the door opens, the sound of hooves engulfs him.

The jockey urges him on—and the instincts he has been bred to know take over. He is a racehorse.

The brooding D. H. Lawrence knew the horse and understood its fondling stroke upon the human spirit: "Far back, far back, in our dark soul the horse prances. . . . The horse, the horse! The symbol of surging potency and power of movement, of action, in man."

No matter how often the sight of an exalted racehorse slices across the senses, the impact is not diminished. "Surging potency" indeed is what Secretariat embodied on

A prospective buyer examines a yearling's foot and leg at the Keeneland yearling sales, after
having decided the horse's pedigree called for a closer look. The colt will be led past
as many times as the observer needs to make a judgment on the horse's conformation. Handling the
legs will provide more evidence. The angle of the pastern should be about
forty-five degrees and the legs should not only be straight but symmetrical; the knees should be
neither too far forward or back; hooves should have good, wide heels;
and hocks should be neither cowed nor sickled.

a dark afternoon in Toronto. He was the hero of heroes, and he had come to the lovely Woodbine track to make the last start of his career. The Triple Crown winner nonpareil, he was a horse among horses who would send youths leaping across the rail in a frenzy to be near greatness.

After his Triple Crown spring, Secretariat had proven—as do all horses—that presumptions of victory need be tempered with acceptance of the rules of nature. No horse is unbeatable, and even those few who have gone unbeaten through their entire careers had their close calls. Ribot was tested at two, and the champion filly Personal Ensign was called upon for the most grinding effort of her life in the Breeder's Cup Distaff to wrest victory by a nostril in the last deep furlong of her career.

Secretariat had lost twice after the Triple Crown. In the Whitney Stakes at Saratoga, he was beaten by a long-shot named Onion—as if the fates had decided that all these

humans forgetting their lessons needed a good mocking to go with their reminder. Secretariat's trainer was the French Canadian Lucien Laurin. Just as Laurin's face could outshine neon in the flash of victory, his countenance on the day after the Whitney shown a despondency that made the reporters' task a sorry one.

Inside his stall, Secretariat stood with his massive haunches facing the door—a sick horse, or maybe just a mad one. Saratoga is known as The Graveyard of Champions, and the winner of the Whitney, after all, was trained by the master of upsets, Allen Jerkens. Still, Secretariat in his deliberate stillness bespoke a raging anger at whatever forces had decreed that he be shown up as mortal.

There came soon more rapid pendulum swings in the career of Secretariat. A world-record performance followed first, in a meeting of champions in the first Marlboro Cup. Even his swift sword of a stablemate, Riva Ridge—older by one year and himself a winner of the

The space of a stallion paddock seems smaller when filled with the spirited presence of Secretariat. Bold Ruler's precocious chestnut son became a well-established sire in his own right, standing at Claiborne with a full book, siring such champions as Lady's Secret—the 1986 Horse of the Year, and Risen Star—winner of the Preakness and Belmont Stakes in 1988.

Derby and Belmont—could not contain the stretch kick of Secretariat. Then defeat came again at the hands of a Jerkens horse. This time it was the chestnut colt Prove Out who ran away from Secretariat, in the Woodward Stakes.

Moved to a grass race for the first time, Secretariat then played upon the public's tendency to compare him to a "Big Red" of long ago. He rushed again through the stretch at Belmont Park to win a race named in honor of a distant Titan. The race was called the Man o' War.

So it was that Secretariat came to the paddock of Woodbine. His regular jockey was Canadian-born Ron Turcotte, who had been suspended for an infraction in a race at Belmont Park. As is customary, stewards at Woodbine felt obliged to observe the suspension as well. Thus, the Canadian-born rider would not be aboard Secretariat in the great horse's only race on Canadian soil. (That we felt such sympathy for Turcotte that day seemed haunting, wasted, a few years later when a spill consigned him to a wheelchair.)

Laurin, the French Canadian who had begun his career scuffling along the circuits of Quebec, chose as Turcotte's replacement the young Eddie Maple. To be entrusted with Secretariat's final performance was an honor not without pressure. A miscue that day would have followed Maple the rest of his career, just as Bill Shoemaker could never erase the day he stood up at the sixteenth pole and (perhaps) blew the Kentucky Derby on Gallant Man.

Ashen-faced, Maple sat aboard Secretariat as they were led from the paddock. Cold wind and slashing rain vied for their attention with an eddy of noisy fans. "The horse, the horse!" had mankind in his spell once more.

They would return in utter triumph. Through the darkening afternoon, Secretariat had rolled alone in the stretch run. The hooded head puffed vapor visibly with every stride, so that the "surging potency" of his species seemed to hark back to some less familiar creature—beautiful of aspect, and a little frightful.

A PHOTOGRAPHIC JOURNAL

In foal to Spectacular Bid, the mare Tuerta grazes contentedly several days before giving birth. Normal gestation lasts an average of 336 days—a bit more than eleven months—but can vary by as much as a few weeks.

PRECEDING PAGE:
Gild, a talented daughter of Mr. Prospector who won the Gardenia Stakes at two, stands over her brand-new filly sired by the brilliant Devil's Bag.

In the spacious box of the foaling stall the mare Cope of Flowers nuzzles her colt, sired by Mr. Prospector, leading sire of 1988. The foal, who weighed about eighty pounds at birth, would gain two pounds a day during his first month on a diet of mare's milk—including the vital colostrum the mare supplies on the first day, which supplies the foal with crucial antibodies—as well as a little clover and bluegrass.

Mare and foal in their stall, the morning after birth. In less than twenty-four hours after it's
born, the foal is fitted with a halter so it can be turned out with his mother for
several hours of sunshine. A day alone at the foaling barn is followed by a move for the
pair to the nursery barn, still under careful observation by the broodmare staff. If all goes
well they'll then join a group of ten or eleven other mares and foals until weaning time.

A winter foal stays right with its mother as she trots through an early snow, the boundaries of the pasture delineated only by the dark rails of the fencing. As racehorses observe a universal birthday, January 1, breeding schedules try to produce foals born before June, so they'll reach considerable size by the late summer or early fall. Those born in the winter will also have more time to mature.

What keeps a foal running behind his mother as she gallops for the creek is surely based on a
bond he'll outgrow. As foals get older and more confident of their own legs,
some will try not just to keep up with their dam, but to pass her—
early training in the art
of racing, taught simply by instinct.

Mares and foals at Cherry Valley. Breeding season finds the population of some farms doubled by the boarders taken on, while other farms keep their populations steady. All the mares are treated with the same constant care.

To satisfy the eager hopes of his owners, this six-week-old foal steps proudly at the leading
of his handler. His dam is close by (although out of the picture),
a reassuring presence during what may be the first time the foal is led on
his own, away from the side of his mother.

The racemare Amber Ever gave birth to this chestnut colt who is practicing a maneuver that
will become tougher to perform as his body assumes the proportions of
maturity. Even the triangular star on his brow will change its relative proportion to
his head, staying the same size while the horse grows.

A bed of clover surrounds this Vaguely Noble filly out of Quill, who at nine days old is
resting up for another series of bursts of energy and frequent canters through the fields with
her dam. She was later named Last Feather—referring, as many racehorse names do,
to the name of her dam—and went on to become a stakes winner in England.

A colt sired by Danzig out of the mare Unity Hall rests in the afternoon sun. Although his
knees and hocks still bear the knobbiness of young legs he's lost his suckling whiskers
and is starting to show the beginnings of muscles that will develop with every bound and
gallop. By now he's probably familiar with his handlers, having had enough gentle
contact that a trip to the weaning center won't be fraught with surprises.

Imparting her offspring with the undeniable urge to run, the graded-stakes winner Tallahto
leads her 1984 filly, Shy Light, on a gallop. The winner of major stakes, Tallahto
carries the speed of paternal grandsire Nasrullah and traces back to the fast-breaking Sir
Gallahad III, whose legacy includes dependably sound legs and feet. Shy Light,
sired by Tom Rolfe, won two races in her third year.

Assistant broodmare foreman Ivan Logan with a well-groomed Jack, one of the teasers used to find out if a mare is "showing," or ready to breed. Brought into the field or up to mares in the barns, the pony stallion would either get a welcome or a hostile reception. On occasion Jack is bred himself to one of the nurse mares usually used for foals who've been orphaned, or whose dams are having trouble producing vital milk.

To accomplish the weaning of as many as 200 foals in one day, Claiborne requires a force of
sixty, from the farm's president Seth Hancock and general manager John Sosby to the
highly experienced staff. Here, head broodmare man Gus Koch supervises as his men push
a strapping seven-month-old weanling onto the van that will take it to its new home
at Raceland. Some foals panic and the risk of injury is high. The two-horse vans are crowded
with five or six weanlings to restrict movement, and after his trip each weanling is
eased off the van and into his stall under careful watch.

Rather than break the spirit that keeps horses running, most handlers prefer a distraction—
such as a lip twitch—to divert the horse's attention and avoid a struggle. At times a
horse is so excited that a twitch is required just to keep him standing still. This yearling is
being restrained with a harmless rope twitch on his upper lip. Great care has been
taken to make sure the twitch doesn't come in contact with the sensitive inner lips.

Six bays and two chestnuts (as the great breeder Frederico Tesio discovered, bays coats are
two-thirds more common in Thoroughbreds than chestnut coats) quench their thirst
in the heat of an Indian-summer afternoon. Turned out in a big field at the yearling farm,
they act like a juvenile herd, with leaders and followers, sometimes taking turns: if
one starts heading for the water tank, the others will follow. With little to do but run, play,
eat, drink, and sleep, they'll grow and develop a great deal in this time. Facing the
arduous process of breaking in less than six months, they'll need their new strength.

With its shady overhang and spacious stalls, the stud barn at Claiborne has proven more than
comfortable for some very particular stallions. The farm now stands twenty-five
stallions a year; many of their predecessors—Nasrullah and Round Table among them—
having proved to be major influences on the breed. From the beginning, founder
Arthur B. Hancock, Sr., paid great attention to having quality sires, and as Claiborne gained
a reputation for being an outstanding breeding operation, other key players began to
take an interest in standing their stallions there.

The buddy system is common to any herd. Here, two yearlings follow each other through a snowstorm which has all but obliterated the surrounding landscape of their rolling pasture.

An old hand at the routines of Claiborne, Spectacular Bid stands at the gate of his two-acre paddock in the morning, waiting for his groom to bring him into the cool barn for the day. Throughout the summer months stallions go on vacation from their breeding schedule, leading a life of habit and leisure.

After a solitary trip to a choice patch of grass on the other side of the stream, this Claiborne yearling heads back across the water to rejoin her filly friends. Most yearling trainers schedule breaking and training time in the mornings, turning their pupils out in the fields in the evenings to get out their kicks in the wide open spaces.

A morning shower is enjoyed by the stallion Tom Rolfe, winner of the Preakness, the
Chicagoan Stakes, the Arlington Classic, and the American Derby at Arlington Park in 1965,
and the 1966 Aqueduct Handicap under Bill Shoemaker. Tom Rolfe now ranks as one
of the leading broodmare sires in the country, standing at stud well into his twenties. Among
his most famous grandchildren is the champion Forty Niner.

Of the two yearlings roughhousing here, the aggressor is clearly the lighter chestnut, who is
more heavily muscled than his counterpart. Yearling fillies, in general less
boisterous than colts, are kept together in a different field. To prep yearlings shortly before
the sales, they'll be separated from their peers and turned out in
individual paddocks—one measure of prevention against the nicks and
scratches that roughhousing so commonly causes.

A bucking rebuff from the lighter bay yearling expresses his exasperation with his dark bay
companion, who was known in that group of yearlings as a bully, his aggression
sparking many confrontations. To keep yearlings evenly matched they're banded according
to age and sex: the oldest stay with the oldest and the youngest with the youngest.

Muscling up fast but still as frisky as teenagers, these two chestnuts are just playing, their rambunctious moods evenly matched. If a play fight escalates into a genuine conflict, one horse will usually back down.

This set of yearlings has been tacked up and led around the shedrow to insure the girth
is properly adjusted and not too tight. The riders, who are waiting to be given
a leg up, will recheck their tack once more before going to the racetrack.

Lulled into a sphinxlike drowsiness by the afternoon sun, a ginger tabby keeps watch from a
weathered barn doorway. Although breeding Thoroughbreds is a complex
business with charts and contracts, computerized databases, and advanced degrees, the
atmosphere around the horse barns is kept as soothing, structured, and quiet as possible.

Popeye, a wirehaired Jack Russell terrier owned by a groom who works for Woody Stephens, spends
his midafternoon hours in the straw. During busy mornings at the track
dogs are usually kept inside; they wait for the afternoon slowdown when they can come out.

A lighter moment for winning trainer Angel Penna (left), and Dr. Pepper at the Saratoga Dog
Show, a fund-raiser for the Thoroughbred Retirement Foundation awarding
prizes for all. Argentinian Penna was inducted into the Racing Hall of Fame in 1988. The
most difficult part of a trainer's job, he has said, is "explaining losing to
owners." As he makes the rounds in his maintenance truck, ex-football player Bruce Bozick
(right), is accompanied by his Labrador retriever puppy C. J.

Claiborne fixtures enjoying the easy life: semiretired Claiborne veteran Frank Kookendoffer passes a friendly moment with Dot, one of the Hancocks' yellow Labrador retrievers.

A close-up look at the small and delicate hoof of champion Spectacular Bid held between the
chaps of the farrier as he pulls off an old shoe. Regular visits from the blacksmith are
vital in maintaining not just the health of the horse's feet, but his performance as well. An ill-
fitting plate could hamper his gait, or, in the case of a breeding stallion such as Bid,
here thirteen years old, hamper his willingness to perform his duties as a stud.

As the farrier trims down his other front foot, the horse Bill Shoemaker called the best he's ever ridden continues to stand calmly, framed by the white-and-yellow doors of the Claiborne barn. The list of wins in Spectacular Bid's amazing career includes the Kentucky Derby, the Preakness, the Meadowlands Cup, and the Marlboro Cup in 1979; and the Santa Anita Handicap, the Haskell, and the Woodward Stakes in 1980. After being syndicated for a record $22 million, the stallion has proved himself a sire of winners.

A bid reflects far more than a first glance. Armed with sales catalogs giving a yearling's lineage for three generations back, including performance records, prospective buyers examine the yearlings before the sale—or send their agents. The bid of $775,000 offered for this promising-looking colt at the Keeneland Sales climbed still higher, all based on a complex mix of highly educated conjecture and straightforward science. Whether or not the colt would live up to his promise, only time would tell.

As tuxedoed spotters keep discreet but clear track of the bids, yearling #188 turns for prospective buyers at the Saratoga summer select sales, which take place during the August race meeting. Along with Keeneland, the auction offers racing's premier yearlings. The youngsters arrive well prepped, having been exposed to varying degrees of handling but always a generous feeding and grooming schedule.

Stud groom Clay Arnold leads Private Account down the path between the paddock to the
barn for the day. Awaiting the stallion is a well-bedded stall with new straw,
a shaking of hay, fresh water, and a measure of the grain mixture Claiborne feeds its horses.
The quantity of feed given will depend on whether or not the stallion is on
active stud duty and how much grass is growing that time of year. This highly valued sire has
frequently made the leading sires list for his progeny of some 272
foals, including the undefeated Personal Ensign.

Before sunrise a groom leads his horse off the van towards a new barn. The horse is
still wearing shipping bandages and may have flown all the way across
the country. Racehorses, given a year-round schedule of racing and
conditioning, become inveterate commuters.

As part of their education, these two year olds are cantered side by side to prevent them
from shying away from other horses in a race. Alternately, they will be galloped
single file to teach them to rate, dropping back from the lead.

The graded stakes-placed Grantley, a five-year-old gelding with a dappled gray coat, enjoys a
light gallop during his freshening-up at the Aiken Training Center in South
Carolina. As is the case with many older campaigners, Grantley needed a season to get ready
for upcoming races at Keeneland. He's been brought along again
with the respect a veteran deserves, having withstood the rigors of a long career.

Between the barns and the grandstand at Hialeah Park in Florida is a pine-shaded lane, a
tranquil route for horses on their way to the morning's work on the track or the
saddling paddock for an afternoon race. Hialeah, the grande dame of Florida tracks, ushered
in a new era of year-round racing in 1925, when for the first time owners
could ship their stables south for a warm season.

Still blowing from the effort, a horse returns from the track at Aiken after a breeze. The best horses go out the earliest, when the air's still cool and the racetrack still fresh, its sand-and-dirt surface not yet chopped up by traffic. Most tracks have to take a midmorning break to reharrow before more galloping can resume.

With the Gulfstream Gap behind him, a young horse goes out to the track for an early
morning gallop. The Hallandale, Florida track is a winter haven for horses, shipped south by
their trainers to keep them in shape and running. Gulfstream Park's most famous race
is the Florida Derby, held in late March. Like Keeneland's Bluegrass Stakes it's one of the
major early tests for three-year-old colts headed for Churchill Downs in May.

The Aiken Trials, held each March at the Aiken Training Center in South Carolina, are a
graduation of sorts for some of the many two-year-olds completing their early
training there. Among the early talent to recently emerge victorious at the trials was
Dogwood Stable's Summer Squall, the winner of the 1990 Preakness Stakes.

At Saratoga a young racehorse with his jockey in the irons gallops alongside a stable pony, getting ready to break off for a fast work. Those observing from the rail will be sure to take note, since jockeys rarely exercise the horses unless a fast work is scheduled —prepping the animal for an upcoming race.

The moon is still overhead at 5:30 the morning after the 1989 eclipse, when a horse in the first set on the Saratoga training track goes out in the quiet company of his stable pony. Some horses develop a dependence on their stable ponies, unable to settle down without them.

A solitary horse gallops in the fog at Keeneland Race Course, adding to the countless miles it
will cover while prepping for one of Keeneland's stakes races. "The sport of racing is
the heritage of Kentuckians," the Keeneland Association declared in 1935, outlining the need
for a new racetrack near Lexington, built on land bought by scion James R. Keene.
The result, opened in 1935, is a model of the old, less-commercial traditions of racing.

In training for the 1978 Bluegrass Stakes—which he won—Calumet Farms' Alydar breaks in
the newly harrowed track at Keeneland Race Course. His exercise rider keeps a
firm—but not restricting—grip on the reins, following the trainer's instructions to let the
big horse travel in the controlled speed between an everyday gallop and racing strides.

The galloping schedule of a horse (this one is moving down the Oklahoma training track at
Saratoga) depends on the trainer's preferences and goals. If a horse has a major work
or runs in a race, the next morning he will be hand walked to give him a rest. Otherwise,
daily morning gallops are vital in maintaining condition.

The sun has barely burned off the early morning's mist as a hot walker takes his horse in the counterclockwise journey around the walking ring at Saratoga. Forty minutes of slow, quiet steps with a few stops for a sip of water usually brings an overheated horse back to a normal, resting pulse.

Dirt and grit could irritate a leg's sensitive skin, a wrinkle could cause a bruise, too much
wear and the bandage won't hold. Given these conditions, grooms keep busy
cleaning and maintaining their horses' wrappings. The sight of white bandages hanging
out to dry is ubiquitous at any track's backstretch, as is the sight of clean
bandages sitting rolled in a tub, ready to be used again.

A fresh box of racing plates in ultralight aluminum, a trimming knife, a rasp, a hoofpick,
pincers, and a clinch are some of the tools found in the blacksmith's box. Racing
horses are shod frequently; the great trainer Woody Stephens believes in having his horse's
feet trimmed at least once a month. Reshoeing a horse every three weeks is not unusual if the animal is
racing or in active training, and trying out different types of shoes
is common if the horse has a conformation flaw that affects his gait.

The leggy filly Add, by Spectacular Bid out of Number, is turned around by her
exercise rider before a gallop at Churchill Downs.

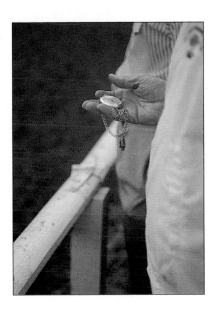

The stopwatch is so often found in a trainer's hand that it almost becomes a part of it. Hall of Fame trainer Mackenzie Miller, now in charge of Rokeby Stable's horses, clocks in his charges at Saratoga. A furlong (⅛ of a mile) in twelve seconds is considered a median; anything more is slow, anything less is fast.

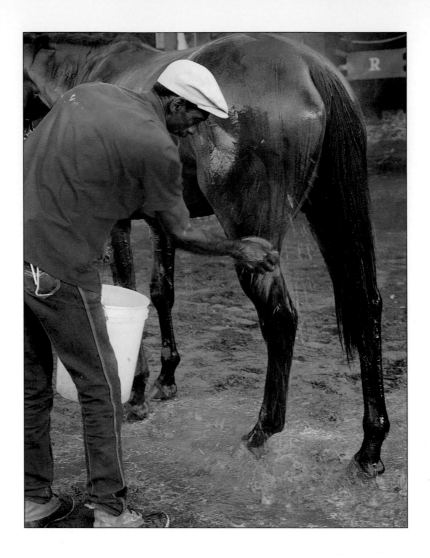

In contact with his charges more than anyone else at the track, this groom from Paul Mellon's
Rokeby Stable is often the first to notice any problems a horse might
have, from being off his feed to showing heat in a leg—
a common sign of an injury. Any deviation from the norm and he'll notify
the trainer. After a workout on a hot day, this bay gets a thorough bath, all the while being
checked for any signs of swelling or scratches as he's sponged down.

Following the bath and a short cooling out the horse is bandaged, a crucial weapon in the battle against the leg injuries that plague some fragile-limbed runners. The wrap is snug enough to stay on but not too tight, and must be even: putting too much stress on one side of the leg could bow a tendon. The run-down bandages put on horses about to race or work are much tighter, as their job is one of support.

Training chart in his lap and phone in his hand, the trainer Shug McGaughey takes notes on his barn's morning works while keeping an eye on the activity of the shedrow. His perpetual involvement has given him an unerring sense of the readiness of his horses, crucial to the many successes he has had while working for the Phipps stable.

Adjacent to the Saratoga racetrack is the Greentree property, where horses can work privately
in the proximity, but without the publicity, of the great racetrack. Here a warm
day's exercise ends with baths near the barn.

The champion two-year-old of 1987, Forty Niner is known around the barn as a kind-hearted horse, always willing to give up the top of his haynet for Trotsek the cat. A constant presence around the barn, this tabby often seeks the company of the colt, while avoiding— as most cats do—the more skittish horses in the barn.

The wonderful Swale, a son of Seattle Slew who won the 1984 Kentucky Derby and Belmont
stakes in powerfully fluid style, sticks his tongue out after a sip of water as his
grooms put a fly sheet on him to keep him unbothered after his bath. Although Swale's
career was cut short by his untimely death, he is widely remembered
for his mellow character—including a phenomenal ability to fall asleep after a
strenuous workout—as much as for his clear talent.

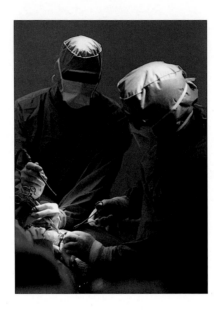

Renowned veterinary surgeon Dr. Robert Copelan performs a bone-chip removal on the knee
of a racehorse. A type of fracture common in horses that are heavily raced and
trained, bone chips occur in joints that are excessively stressed, overextended, or just tired.
Through advances in techniques and equipment, injuries that used to prove
fatal now frequently can be repaired, at times enabling a horse to return to the track.

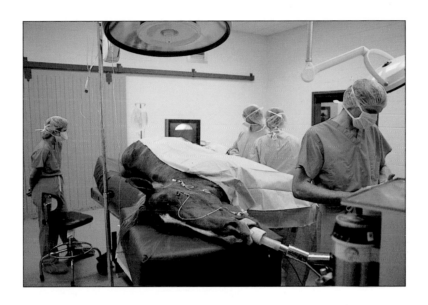

Internationally respected for his work in arthroscopic surgery, Dr. Larry Bramladge works on removing a bone chip from a horse in an operating room at Rood and Riddle Equine Hospital in Lexington, Kentucky.

A groom hoses down the strong but slender legs of champion Easy Goer after a strenuous
work. Retired in his fourth year after a bone chip was found in his right
front ankle, the powerful son of Alydar stayed sound enough to earn $4,873,770 in
purse money throughout his two-year career. He is now standing at
Claiborne, where he was bred and raised.

Hydrotherapy is another advance in equine veterinary care: swimming can provide a horse
with vigorous exercise without placing stress on his limbs, a crucial factor in
the recovery of many leg injuries. The 1983 Belmont Stakes winner Caveat was assigned to
a program of daily swimming after he injured a tendon. Phil Gleaves, the
assistant trainer to Woody Stephens, leads Caveat through his circular laps.

Some of Pat Day's rides should be proof enough that a jockey's ride is anything but a "just
hold on" proposition. His strategic riding of the exuberant Easy Goer in the
1989 Belmont brought the colt home with an eight-length lead, and his patient urging helped
Tank's Prospect take the 1985 Preakness with an impressive come-from-behind
rally. Day's stamina is becoming legendary: known for being willing to ride race after race,
he won eight out of nine races at Arlington International in Illinois on September 13, 1989.

World champion Angel Cordero, Jr., has guided more than 6,000 horses to a winning finish
with his agressive riding, including Bold Forbes in the 1976 Belmont and
Cannonade in the 1974 Kentucky Derby. A picture of confidence in the saddling
paddock, Cordero is waiting for last-minute instructions from the
trainer before he gets in the irons for Belmont's next race. The three sets of goggles
he's wearing will all get used: as one gets spattered with the mud and dirt that flies up during
the race, he'll pull it down and switch to the one underneath.

Another jockey to emerge on the forefront is the powerful Julie Krone, now ranked the
premier female jockey and on the rise again after an arm fracture in 1989. A favorite of
many trainers in the New York and New Jersey area, she's known for both her strength and her ability to
bring a horse home in the money through a combination of
balancing, rating (adjusting the horse's stride), coaxing, and urging.

A trim José Santos, leading money rider in 1986, 1987, 1988, and 1989, turns toward a
conversation in the saddling paddock before a race in Kentucky. His winning
streak at Saratoga in 1987 earned him that year's riding title.

A yellow sweep of silks in the silks room, where the jockey's uniforms are hung with care
according to their primary colors, from yellow to black, hot pink to neon green,
some hearkening back to the track's Victorian history.

A thoroughly modern seat and thoroughly modern materials: aluminum stirrups—
still called irons with a nod towards racing's history, ultralight nylon
breeches, rubber reins. Having just finished tying the knot in his reins for a better
hold, this jockey sits back in the saddle, keeping his whip still as he
rides to the post. The modern seat, originated in 1903 by the British jockey Tod Sloan,
places the weight of the jockey far above the horse's withers and frees his hands.

Amid the sunshine and palms the call, "riders up" goes out, and jockeys begin to mount for
the next race at Del Mar. Singer Bing Crosby and actor Pat O'Brien helped to found
this southern California racetrack in 1937 with a blend of Hollywood elegance and California
informality. Fans are a minute or two from the Pacific Ocean, and the mission-style
architecture has the open feel of a beach house.

The sinewy lines of Newstead Farm's Miss Oceana are highlighted in the afternoon sun as she
heads from the saddling paddock to a race. The walk gives the betting public a chance
to review their decisions, gives the jockey—here Eddie Maple—a last chance to adjust his
reins and get his seat right, and gives a fit horse a chance to accumulate even more
pent-up energy in close anticipation of the race.

Science, luck, proverbs, and prayers: wagering on horses is a game in which everyone plays, since the bettors create the odds (thus the phrase "odds-on money favorite," in which a star runner would pay less than even money if he won). The odds board begins with numbers established by an astute linemaker, who anticipates the slant of the betting and displays the results on the morning line. As bettors begin to place their money, the numbers displayed on the odds board (this one's at Saratoga) change, and will continue to change right up to the minute before a race.

Handicappers form an elite coterie of myserious experts—mysterious since the formulas an outstanding handicapper employs are as secret as Grandma's recipe for mincemeat. Saratoga's handicappers congregate at the Jim Dandy bar, where, drink in one hand and *Racing Form* in the other, they compare notes with the rigor of academicians.

To the post: Sunday Silence, with Pat Valenzuela up, is led by his groom from the saddling
paddock to the track, where a red-coated outrider is waiting to head the
parade of horses and jockeys to the gate for the start of the Hollywood Gold Cup. This
son of Halo enjoyed a highly successful career, taking the Horse of the
Year title in 1989 after winning the Kentucky Derby, the Preakness Stakes, the
Super Derby, the Breeders' Cup, and others.

Shouting encouragement to their surging mounts, jockeys vie for position after exploding from
the starting gate at Keeneland. Taking a good position early on is vital. A jockey on a
horse that likes to come from behind will try to tuck behind the frontrunners and lie off the
pace, conserving the horse's energy for a final drive. A jockey on a frontrunner will
urge his horse forward and try to snatch a good position on the inside rail. A good jockey can
keep track of seconds, even fractions going by, and can draw on experience—
and courage—to make the right maneuver.

Passing the quarter-mile pole, a closely bunched field
rounds the turn in a spring race at Keeneland.

Among the physical factors that enable Thoroughbreds to maintain sheer speed over distance
are their powerful hearts, which send a fifteenth of the total volume of their blood
surging through their arteries with each beat.

Turf specialists get their chance during a race at Saratoga, with the old Saratoga grandstand
behind the field. Certain horses excel on the turf and enjoy successful campaigns in
Europe, where most races are run on grass. Rarely are horses versatile enough to race on both
grass and dirt; the great gelding John Henry was a game and talented exception.

Both riders go to the whip, urging their horses to summon a last burst of speed during
a climactic run down the front stretch. It's the last furlong of a
turf race at Santa Anita, and horse #1, on the rail, is fighting to keep his
lead as a blinkered #8 surges toward the finish.

Panama-born Laffit Pincay, Jr., leads the list of racing's money-winning riders, with a
cumulative total of $148 million through 1989. Pincay is known for his
unbelievable strength in the stretch, as well as for his self-discipline—
his restraint at a meal has impressed many a trainer. His power has garnered him victories
in more than 7,000 races (following Bill Shoemaker)— among them, Swale's
winning of the 1984 Kentucky Derby and the Belmont Stakes. Pincay holds a record
five Eclipse Awards and was elected to the Racing Hall of Fame in 1975.

Stepping off a moving horse and onto the scales can be a moment of doubt for any jockey.
Jockeys are required to weigh in with saddle and pads at the start of each race
and weigh out at the finish. Standard weight allowances require many jockeys to maintain
a racing weight of 112 pounds or below—easy for some, a constant struggle for others,
particularly since he, or she, must be disproportionately strong.

Following Go For Wand's victory in the 1990 Alabama Stakes at Saratoga, all involved with
the filly, from family to stable help, joined owner Mrs. Jane DuPont Lunger and
trainer William Badgett in the Winner's Circle to celebrate. Winner of the Mother Goose
Stakes at Belmont, the filly was the outstanding distaff runner of 1990—
evidence of bloodlines that trace back, on her father's side, to the brilliant Nearctic,
and on her mother's side, to the great Count Fleet.

The Claiborne trophies include the long sought-after Kentucky Derby and Belmont
trophies as well as the cherished Keeneland cups, tray, and pitcher. Six
stakes wins the tray, six more the pitcher—Claiborne has four of the next six necessary
for the coveted, and as of yet unawarded, Keeneland Bowl.

Banners portraying the Triple Crown champions festoon the oval hall
of the Kentucky Derby Museum in Louisville.

Shortly after Secretariat's death at the age of nineteen, many of his fans—
most of whom were unknown to the racing
world—sent flowers for Claiborne Farm to place at his grave.

To most American horse-owners, there is no trophy more coveted than a Kentucky Derby
trophy engraved with the name of their horse.

APPENDIX

SELECTED HORSE FARMS

AIRDRIE/WOODBURN

P.O. Box 487
Midway, KY 40347

Best thoroughbreds bred: Imp
Society, Silver Medallion, By
Land by Sea

AKINDALE

Quaker Hill Road
Pawling, NY 12564

Farm acquired: 1944; established
as a thoroughbred farm: 1974
Original farm 44 acres, now 420
Biggest accomplishment: Breeding
Stakes Winners: Jazzing
Around, Warfie, Yestday's
Kisses
Sales: $550,000 yearling by
Deputy Minister-La Belle Fleur
in 1987

ASHFORD STUD

P.O. Box 823
Versailles, KY 40383

Farm established 1979, acquired
by present owner 1984
Champions bred or raised on
farm: Indian Skimmer
Presently standing stallions:
Storm Bird, Woodman

BROOKMEADE

Upperville, VA

Founded by Mrs. Isabel Dodge
Sloane; now owned by Joseph
Albritton and operated as Lazy
Lane Farm.
Present acreage: 850
Mrs. Sloane bred 63 stakes
winners including: Inlander,
(Leading money winning 3
year old of 1933) champion
Cavalcade (won Kentucky
Derby), Sword Dancer (Horse
of the Year in 1959), Bowl of
Flowers (best filly at 2 and 3).

BROOKSIDE FARM

Route 1 Steele Road
Versailles, KY 40383

Farm acquired: 1984
Present acreage: 1600 acres
Has won Eclipse Awards with
purchased horses: Estrapade,
Blushing John, Theatrical

BUCKRAM OAK FARM

3530 Old Frankfort Pike
Lexington, KY 40510

Farm established: 1979
Present acreage: 470 acres
Buckram Oaks Holdings, N.V.
races thoroughbreds in France,
England and the United States.

Best thoroughbreds bred: Lady in
Silver, Three Generations, Pearl
Bracelet, Fast Topaze, etc.

CALUMET

3301 Versailles Road
Lexington, KY 40510

Best thoroughbreds bred and
raced: Citation, Armed,
Bewitch, Whirlaway, Alydar,
Criminal Type, etc.
Farm acreage: 849 acres

CARDIFF STUD FARM

P.O. Box 310
Creston, CA 93432

Farm acreage: 1200 acres
Best thoroughbreds bred: The
Carpenter, Croeso, Shywing,
River Master
Best thoroughbreds raced:
Caucasus, King Pellinore, The
Carpenter, Desert Wine, River
Master

CLAIBORNE FARMS, INC.

Rt. #2, Winchester Road
P.O. Box 150
Paris, KY 40361

Best thoroughbreds bred and
raced: Bayou, Coastal, Delta,
Dike, Dunce, Doubledogdare,
Forty Niner, Moccasin, Round
Table, Swale

Best thoroughbreds sold at
auction: Caerleon, Cellini,
Ivanijica, Nureyev, Royal
Glint, Sham, Wajima
Farm acreage: 3500 acres—since
1908
Champion thoroughbreds raised
for others: Apalachee, Bold
Lad, Bold Ruler, Buckpasser,
Chief's Crown, Dahlia,
Revidere, Easy Goer, Forego,
Ferdinand, Gamely, Lamb
Chop, Personal Ensign, Queen
Empress, Relaxing, Reviewer,
Rhythm, Ruffian, Shahraastani,
Slew of Gold, Go for Wand,
Vitriolic, etc.
Stallions which have stood at
Clairborne who have sired
champions: Blenheim II, Bold
Ruler, Buckpasser, Cox's
Ridge, Damascus, Danzig,
Gallant Fox, Mr. Prospector,
Nasrullah, Nijinsky II, Private
Account, Princequillo,
Secretariat, Tom Rolfe, etc.

DARBY DAN FARM

3225 Old Frankfort Pike
Lexington, KY 40510

Best thoroughbreds bred and
raced: Chateaugay, Proud
Clarion, Primonetta, Bramalea,
Roberto, Little Current,
Graustark, His Majesty, Maud

Muller, Java Moon, Grenfall, True Knight, Candalita, Cum Laude Laurie, Good Counsel, Hail the Pirates, Black Beard, Boundless, Clear Dawn, Evening Time, Summer Air, Sylvan Place, Up Scope, Skipper Bill, Infuriator, Narrissa, Prince Dantar, Prince Thou Art, Proud Truth, Sunshine Forever.
Kentucky farm: 648 acres
Ohio farm: established in 1935 with 110 acres. Today has 4200 acres

ELMENDORF

3931 Paris Pike
Lexington, KY 40509

Farm established: 1897, acquired January 1, 1985 by Jack Kent Cooke
Present acreage: 503
Best thoroughbreds bred and raced: Protagonist, Talking Picture, Big Spruce, Verbatim, Manta, Specious, Girl in Love, Spout, Improvisor, Drama Critic, Pay Tribute, Harvest Girl, Magazine, Sweet Old Girl, Free Journey, Text, Road Princess, Rich Soil, Transworld, Lilac Hill, Provante, Sir Jason, Do So, Flying Continental
One of the oldest farms in continuous operation in America.

GAINESWAY FARM

3750 Paris Pike
Lexington, KY 40511

Farm acreage: 500 acres
Purchased by Graham Beck in 1988

GAINSBOROUGH FARM

Route #1 Steele Road
Versailles, KY 40383

Present acreage: 780
Acquired: 1984

GREENTREE STUD

Room 4600
110 West 51st Street
New York, New York 10020

Best thoroughbreds bred and raced: The Axe II, Stage Door Johnny, Stop the Music, Devil Diver, Shut Out, Twenty Grand, Capot, Cyrano, Bowl Game, Late Bloomer, Open Call
Best thoroughbred bought and raced: Tom Fool
Farm acreage sold to Graham Beck 1989; Mr. John II. Whitney retained Greentree name to use for racing stable.

HAGYARD FARM

4913 Paris Pike
Lexington, KY 40511

Best thoroughbreds bred and raced: Rude Awakening, La Gentillesse
Best thoroughbreds raised for others: Hail to Reason, Promised Land, Affectionately, Personality, High Echelon, Allez France, Straight Deal, Priceless Gem, Regal Gleam,

Isle of Greece, Sister Antonie, Palestinian, Journalist, Beau Busher
Best thoroughbreds sold at auction: Rough 'n Tumble, Unbridled, National Anthem, Rising Market, Long Position, King Cole

HAMBURG PLACE

P.O. Box 12128
Lexington, KY 40508-2128

Established 1897—2000 acres
Best thoroughbreds bred: Alysheba, Pink Pigeon, Mairzy Doates, Buffalo Lark, Kentuckian, Miss Carmie
Best thoroughbreds raised for others: Native Charger, Golden Don, Silver Series, Staunch Avenger, El Senor

HERMITAGE FARM, INC.

P.O. Box 40
Goshen, KY 40026

Farm acquired and established in 1935. Present Acreage 860.
Biggest achievement in the history of the farm: Twice sold world's record yearling One Bold Bid (1964 $170,000) Seattle Dancer (1985 $13.1 M.)
Best thoroughbreds bred: King's Bishop, Dark Star (1953 Kentucky Derby), Nancy Jr (1967 Kentucky Oaks), Lomond, Is It True
Best thoroughbreds sold: Dark Star, King's Bishop, Northern Trick, Rousillon, Woodman, Bold Fascinator, Marble Arch

HICKORY TREE

Box 125
Middleburg, VA 22117

Present acreage: 1600
Best thoroughbreds bred: Hagley, Bring Out The Band, Believe It, Terpischorist, Gorytus
Best throughbreds bought and raced: Glad Rags II, Soeree, Choti, Devil's Bag, Gone West

HOBEAU FARM

P.O. Box 70
Ocala, FL 32670

Farm established: 1961
Present acreage: 2280
Best thoroughbreds bred and raced: Beau Purple, Onion, Handsome Boy, Beau Legs, Blessing Angelica, Step Nicely, Duck Dance
Best thoroughbreds bought and raced: Third Martini, Canal, Mac's Sparkler, Prove Out, Poker Night, Peace Corps, Kinsman Hope, Group Plan, Bertee, Chas Conerly, Flip's Pleasure, Kilmonay, Never Bow

HURSTLAND/NUCKOLS

P.O. Box 305
Midway, KY 40347-0305

Best thoroughbreds sold: Typecast, White Skies, Decathlon, Habitat, Broadway Dancer, etc.

INDIAN CREEK

P.O. Box 294 Redmond Road
Paris, KY 40361

Present acreage: 140
Best horse raised: Anifa, Tina
Tina Too
Best horse raised for others: Life's
Magic, Romeo Romani

JONABELL FARM

3333 Bowman's Mill Road
Lexington, KY 40513

Established: 1946
Present acreage: 800
Best thoroughbreds sold at
auction: Syrian Sea; Nijinky
II-Syrian Sea Yrlg. Colt
Champions bred or raised:
Battlefield, Damascus, Green
Forest, Epitome, Miss Gris,
Never Say Die, One For All,
Shicklah, Somethingdifferent
Best raised for others: Damascus,
Bonding Basque, Vigors,
Summing, Honorable Miss,
Highland Blade, Heatherten,
Shy Dawn, Never Say Die,
Etc.

KING RANCH

3000 Old Frankfort Pike
Lexington, KY 40510

Farm acquired from Col.
Bradley's estate (formerly part
of Idle Hour Farm) in 1946
Present Acreage: 670
Best thoroughbreds sold: Solford,
Sadeem, Ensconse

Best thoroughbreds bred: Assault,
Middleground, Gallant Bloom,
Althea, Too Chic, etc.

LANE'S END

Midway Pike
Versailles, KY 40383

Established: 1979
Present acreage: 3,000
Best thoroughbreds bred or
raised: Summer Squall, Bet
Twice, Law Society, Lomond,
Northern Trick, Rousillon,
Sacahuista
Leading consignor at Keeneland
July Selected Yearling Sale
1988, 1989, 1990

LOCUST HILL

Glydon, MD 21071

Best thoroughbreds bred and
raced: Ruffian, Icecapade,
Tyrant, Promise, On Your
Toes, Blue Ensign, Assault
Landing, Steal Maiden, St.
Brendan, Finders Choice,
Wedding Party, Private Terms,
Near East, Buckfinder,
Positively So
Farm acquired in 1936, 400 acres

MILL RIDGE

3414 Bowman's Mill
Lexington, KY 40513

Farm established: 1880, acquired
1962 (part of Beaumont Farm)
Present acreage: 550
Best thoroughbred sold at
auction: Sir Ivor

Best thoroughbreds bred:
Nicosia, Silent Account, Sir
Ivor, Ciao, Trapp Mountain,
Secret Hello, Songlines
Best thoroughbreds bought and
raced: Drumtop and Nicosia

NEWSTEAD

P.O. Box 184
Upperville, VA 22176

Acquired in 1937; owner, Taylor
Hardin, died in 1985.
Best thoroughbreds bred and
sold: True North, Lord Gayle,
Filiberto, Northern Gem,
Sweet Alliance
Best raised for others: Dancing
Champ, War Emperor, Rich
Tradition, Hasty Doll, Sky
Clipper
Best thoroughbreds bred and
raced: Mrs. Warren, Mrs.
Peterkin, Gulls Cry, White Star
Line, Miss Oceana, Landa

OCALA STUD

P.O. Box 818
Ocala, FL 32678

Farm established: 1950, acquired
1956
Present acreage: 500
Best thoroughbred sold at
auction: First Horse of the
Year sold at auction—Roman
Brother
Best thoroughbreds bred or
raised: My Dear Girl, Roman
Brother, Office Queen,
Swinging Mood, Carry Back

OLD ENGLISH RANCHO

1550 E. Locust St.
Ontario, CA 91761

Farm established: 1948
Present acreage: 550
Best thoroughbreds bred: Stylish
Winner, Impressive Style,
Special Warmth, Maginative

PIN OAK FARM

Route 1 US 60/P.O. Box 68
Versailles, KY 40393

Present acreage: 750
Best thoroughbreds bred:
Touching Wood, Elocutionist,
Tree of Knowledge, Roman
Pistol, Laugh and Be Merry

ROKEBY FARMS

Route #1 Box 74
Upperville, VA 22176

Present acreage: 4000
Acquired: 1937
Best thoroughbreds bred and
raced: Arts and Letters, Fort
Marcy, Key to the Mint, Mill
Reef, Run the Gantlet, Silly
Season, Quadrangle, Glowing
Tribute, Java Gold, Hero's
Honor, Winter's Tale

SAGAMORE

3501 Belmont Avenue
Glyndon, MD 21071

Formerly owned by Alfred
Vanderbilt
Present acreage: 560
Best thoroughbreds bred and
raced: Native Dancer, Bed

O'Roses, Find, Miss Disco, Social Outcast, Next Move, Loser Weeper, Petrify, Cold Comfort
Best thoroughbred bought and raced: Discovery

SHADWELL FARM

550 Parkers Mill Road
Lexington, KY 40513

Farm acquired: 1985
Present acreage: 1,500 acres
Best thoroughbred and raced in first crops: Nashwan

SPENDTHRIFT FARM

884 Ironworks Pike
Lexington, KY 40511

Farm established: 1937, acquired present owners 1989
Bred or raised more than 250 stakes winners, including Majestic Prince, Mr. Prospector, Landaluce, Idun, Lucky Lucky Lucky, etc.

STONE FARM

1873 Winchester Road
Paris, KY 40361

Farm established: 1970
Present acreage: 4000 acres
Best thoroughbreds bred or raised: Risen Star, Gato Del Sol, Sunday Silence, Lemhi Gold, Tiffany Lass, Hawaiian Sound
Best thoroughbreds raced: Sunday Silence, Gato Del Sol, Goodbye Halo, Infinidad

SUGAR MAPLE

Route 216 P.O. Box 687
Poughquag, NY 12570

Best thoroughbreds raced: Sir Harry Lewis, Champagneforashley, Distinctive Pro, Maplejinsky

TANRACKIN FARM

Bedford Hills
Westchester County, NY 10507

Farm established: 1941 (inherited from grandfather)
Present acreage: 350
Best thoroughbreds bred and raised: Mr Right, Mustato, Wings of Morning, Without Warning, Restless Feet, Wandering Cloud, Mighty Wonder, Catch the Moon

TARTAN FARMS

6775 SW 43rd Avenue
Ocala, FL 32676

Farm established: 1959, acquired 1959
Present acreage: 1,020
Best thoroughbreds bred or raised: Dr Fager, Ta Wee, Dr Patches, Unbridled, Smile, In Reality, Codex

THE STALLION STATION

6000 Greenwich Pike
Lexington, KY 40511

Best thoroughbreds bred and raced: Two to Paris
Best thoroughbreds bought and raced: Traffic Judge, Alanesian

THREE CHIMNEYS

P.O. Box 114
Old Frankfort Pike
Midway, KY 40347

Best thoroughbred sold at auction: George Navonod
Best thoroughbred bought and sold: A La Dancer
Best thoroughbred bred and raced: Gorgeous

THREE RINGS

P.O. Box 668
Beaumont, CA 92223

Aquired in 1948: over 200 acres
Best thoroughbreds bred by owners: Winds Sands, Crystal Watchers, Today 'n Tomorrow, Just a Kick, Stained Glass, Against the Snow, If You Prefer, Lullaby Song, Brood Shadows.
Best thoroughbreds raised for others: Ancient Title, Painted Wagon, Out of the East, Olive Wreath

WALMAC

3395 Paris Pike
Lexington, KY 40511

Farm established: 1977
Present acreage: 260 (owned), 250-1,100 (leased)
Biggest achievement in the history of the farm:
Sale—Leading consignor of stakes winners sold at Keeneland in 1989.
Leading consignor at 1988 Kenneland Nov. sale.

WINDFIELDS

P.O. Box 67
Oshawa, Ontario
Canada L1H 7KB

Farm established: 1950
Present acreage: 1,250
Best thoroughbreds bred: Nearctic, Northern Dancer, Nijinky II, The Minstrel, Glorious Song, Devil's Bag, Secreto, El Gran Senor, etc.

WOODSTOCK

Chesapeake City, MD, 21915

Farm established: 1953, acquired 1939
Best thoroughbreds bred and raced: Kelso (5 time Horse of the Year), Politely

XALAPA FARM AND TRAINING CENTER

2308 N. Middletown Road
Paris, KY 40361

Year established: 1870, acquired 1915
Present acreage: 2,800
Best thoroughbreds bred: Mate, Mission
Best thoroughbreds raced: Splendid, Spruce, Eternal, One More Bid

BROODMARE OF THE YEAR

1965 POCAHONTAS
(1955, ROMAN-HOW, BY
*PRINCEQUILLO)

Dam of 7 foals including:
Chieftain (1961 c. by Bold Ruler)
13 wins 2 to 4, $405,256, Cowdin
S., Governor's Gold Cup, Arlington H, etc. Sire. Tom Rolfe
(1962 c. by *Ribot) 16 wins 2 to 4,
$671,297, Preakness S., American
Derby, 2nd Belmont S., 3rd Kentucky Derby, etc. Sire.

1966 JULIETS NURSE
(1948, COUNT FLEET-NURSEMAID,
BY LUKE MCLUKE)

Dam of 13 foals including:
Run for Nurse (1957 c. by Hasty
Road) 22 wins $253,145, Chicagoan S., Detroit Sweepstakes H.,
3rd Hawthorne Gold Cup, Sire.
Gallant Romeo (1961 c. by *Gallant Man) 15 wins 2 to 5, $202,401,
Olympia H., Vosburgh H., etc.
Sire. Woozem (1964 f. by Hail to
Reason) 7 wins, $163,083, Demoiselle S., Golden Rod., etc.

1967 KERALA
(1958, *MY BABU-BLADE OF TIME,
BY *SICKLE)

Dam of 13 foals including:
Damascus (1964 c. by Sword
Dancer) 21 wins 2 to 4, $1,176,781,
Preakness S., Belmont S., Wood

Memorial S., Jockey Club Gold
Cup, 3rd Kentucky Derby,
Brooklyn H., etc. Sire.

1968 DELTA
(1952, *NASRULLAH-BOURTAI, BY
STIMULUS)

Dam of 10 foals including:
Canal (1961 g. by Round Table) 33
wins, $280,358, Chicago H.
(twice), Oceanport H. (twice),
Meadowland H., etc. Cabildo
(1963 c. by Round Table) 22 wins,
$267,265, New Orleans H., Midwest H., 2nd Hawthorne Gold
Cup H., etc. Sire. Dike (1966 c. by
*Herbager) 7 wins, $351,274,
Wood Memorial S., Gotham S.,
2nd Travers S., 3rd Belmont S.,
Kentucky Derby, etc. Sire. Also
dam of stakes winners Shore and
Okavango.

1969 ALL BEAUTIFUL
(1959, BATTLEFIELD-PARLO, BY
*HELIOPOLIS)

Dam of 12 foals including:
Arts and Letters (1966 c. by
*Ribot) champion handicap male
in 1969, 1970 and Horse of the
Year in 1969. 11 wins 2 to 5,
$632,404, Belmont S., Travers S.,
Woodward S., 2nd Kentucky
Derby, Preakness S., etc. Sire.

1970 LEVEE
(1953, HILL PRINCE-BOURTAI, BY
STIMULUS)

Dam of 11 foals including:
Nalee (1960 f. by Nashua) 8 wins
at 2 and 3, $141,631, Blue Hen S.,
Black Eyed Susan S., Santa Ynez
S., etc. Royal Gunner (1962 c. by
*Royal Charger) 6 wins 2 to 4,
$334,650, Futurity Trial, 2nd
Woodward S. (twice), Arlington
Classic, etc. Sire. Shuvee (1966 f.
by Nashua) twice champion handicap female, 16 wins 2 to 5,
$890,445, Mother Goose S.,
Acorn S., Jockey Club Gold Cup
(twice), etc. Also dam of stakes
winner A. T.'s Olie.

1971 IBERIA
(1954, *HELIOPOLIS-WAR EAST, BY
*EASTON)

Dam of 10 foals including:
Hydrologist (1966 c. by *Tatan) 10
wins, $277,958, Discovery H.,
Excelsior H., 2nd. Woodward S.,
Whitney S., etc. Riva Ridge (1969
c. by First Landing) 1971 champion 2-year-old colt, 17 wins 2 to
4, $1,111,497, Kentucky Derby,
Belmont S., Hollywood Derby,
Champagne S., etc. Sire. Also dam
of stakes winner Potomac.

1972 *MOMENT OF TRUTH II
(1959, MATADOR-KINGSWORTH, BY
KINGSTONE)

Dam of 9 foals including:
Indulto (1963 g. by Royal Coinage)
27 wins, $466,789, Withers S., Jim
Dandy S., 2nd Great American S.,
etc. Convenience (1968 f. by Fleet
Nasrullah) 15 wins 2 to 5,
$648,933, Vanity H. (twice), 2nd
Santa Margarita Invitational H.,
etc. Also dam of stakes winners
Proliferation, Puntilla.

1973 SOMETHINGROYAL
(1952, *PRINCEQUILLO-
IMPERATRICE, BY CARUSO)

Dam of 17 foals including:
Sir Gaylord (1959 c. by *Turn-To)
10 wins at 2 and 3, $337,404, Sapling, Great American S., 3rd
Champagne S., etc. Sire. First
Family (1962 c. by First Landing) 7
wins 2 to 4, $188,040, Gulf Stream
Park H., 3rd Belmont, etc. Syrian
Sea (1965 f. by Bold Ruler) 6 wins
at 2 and 3, $278,245, Selima S.,
2nd Black Eyed Susan S., 3rd.
Coaching Club American Oaks,
etc. Secretariat (1970 c. by Bold
Ruler) Horse of the Year and
champion at 2 and 3 in 1972 and
1973, Triple Crown winner; 16
wins in 21 starts, $1,316,808, Ken-

tucky Derby, Preakness Stakes, Belmont S., Marlboro Cup H., etc. Sire.

1974 COSMAH
(1953, COSMIC BOMB-ALMAHMOUD, BY *MAHMOUD)

Dam of 15 foals including:
Tosmah (1961 f. by Tim Tam) 1963 champion filly at 2 and 3, 23 wins, 2 to 5, $612,588, Frizette S., Arlington Classic, Matron H., etc. Father's Image (1963 c. by Swaps) 7 wins 2 to 4, $173,318, City of Miami H., 2nd Arlington-Washington Futurity, Cowdin S., etc. Halo (1969 c. by Hail to Reason) 9 wins 2 to 5, $259,553. Lawrence Realization S., United Nations H., 3rd Jersey Derby, etc. Sire. Also dam of stakes winner Maribeau.

1975 SHENANIGANS
(1963, NATIVE DANCER-BOLD IRISH, BY FIGHTING FOX)

Dam of 6 foals, 6 winners, including:
Icecapade (1969 c. by Nearctic) 13 wins 3 to 5, $256,468, Saranac S., Kelso H., 2nd Withers S., etc. Sire. Ruffian (1972 f. by Reviewer) champion filly at 2 and 3, 10 wins in 11 starts, Coaching Club American Oaks, Mother Goose S., Acorn S., etc. Buckfinder (1974 c. by Buckpasser) 9 wins at 3 and 4, $230,513, Celanese Cup H., William DuPont Jr. H., 2nd Metropolitan H., etc. Sire.

1976 *GAZALA II
(1964, DARK STAR-*BELLE ANGEVINE, BY L'AMIRAL)

Dam of 10 foals including:
Mississipian (1971 c. by *Vaguely Noble) champion 2-year-old in France. Winner of $262,322, Grand Criterium, Prix Niel, etc. Sire. Youth (1973 c. by Ack Ack) 8 wins in 11 starts $687,224. Champion grass male of 1976. Won Prix Du Jockey Club, Prix Lupin, Washington Int., etc. Best of Both (1980 c. by J. O. Tobin) Winner of $233,838. Santa Gertrudes H., 2nd Stars and Stripes H., etc. Sire.

1977 SWEET TOOTH
(1965, ON-AND-ON-PLUM CAKE, BY PONDER)

Dam of 11 foals including:
Our Mims (1974 f. by *Herberger) 6 wins, $368,034, Fantasy S., Coaching Club American Oaks, Alabama S., 2nd Kentucky Oaks, etc. Alydar (1975 c. by Raise A Native) 14 wins 2 to 4, $957,195, Florida Derby, Flamingo S., 2nd Kentucky Derby, Preakness S., Belmont S., etc. Sire. Sugar and Spice (1977 f. by Key to the Mint) 5 wins, $257,046, Mother Goose S., Ashland S., 3rd Alabama S., etc.

1978 PRIMONETTA
(1958, SWAPS-BANQUET BELL, BY POLYNESIAN)

Dam of 7 foals including:
Maud Muller (1971 f. Graustark) 3 wins, $138,383, Gazelle, Ashland, 2nd Test S., 3rd Coaching Club

American Oaks, etc. Prince Thou Art (1972 c. by Hail To Reason) 3 wins $167,902, Florida Derby, 2nd Flamingo S., Jim Dandy S., 3rd Travers S., etc. Cum Laude Laurie (1974 f. by Hail To Reason) 8 wins at 3 and 4, $405,207, Beldame S., Ruffian H., Spinster S., etc.

1979 SMARTAIRE
(1962, *QUIBU-ART TEACHER, BY OLYMPIA)

Dam of 12 foals, 10 winners including:
Quadratic (1975 c. by Quadrangle) 6 wins, $233,941, Cowdin S., Everglades S., 2nd Louisiana Derby, 3rd Remsen, etc. Sire. Smarten (1976 c. by Cyane) 11 wins at 2 and 3, $716,426, Illinois Derby, Ohio Derby, American Derby, 2nd Travers S., etc. Sire. Smart Angle (1977 f. by Quadrangle) 1979 champion 2-year-old filly, 7 wins, $414,217, Frizette S., Selima S., Matron S., etc. Smart Heiress (1979 f. by *Vaguely Noble) 6 wins at 2 and 3, $154,999, Garden City S., The Very One S., etc.

1980 KEY BRIDGE
(1959, *PRINCEQUILLO-BLUE BANNER, BY WAR ADMIRAL)

Dam of 11 foals including:
Fort Marcy (1964 g. by *Amerigo) 21 wins 2 to 7, $1,109,791, Washington D.C. Int., Nashua H., Sunset H., Hollywood Park Inv., Turf H., etc. Champion grass horse of 1967, 1970 and champion handicap horse and Horse of the Year in 1970. Key to the Mint (1969 c. by

Graustark) 14 wins 2 to 4, $576,015, Remsen S., Travers S., Woodward S., Whitney S., 3rd Preakness S., etc., Sire. Key To The Kingdom (1970 c. by Bold Ruler) 7 wins $109,590, Stymie H., etc. Sire. Key To Content (1977 c. by *Forli) 7 wins 2 to 4, $354,772, Saranac S., United Nations H., etc.

1981 NATASHKA
(1963, DEDICATE-NATASHA, BY *NASRULLAH)

Dam of 9 foals including:
Truly Bound (1978 f. by In Reality) 9 wins in 12 starts, $382,449, Arlington-Washington Lassie S., Fair Ground Oaks, Governor's Cup., etc. Gregorian (1979 c. by Graustark) 4 wins in 9 starts, $199,369. Sire. Ivory Wand (1973 f. by Sir Ivor) 5 wins in 13 starts, $97,452, Test S.

1982 BEST IN SHOW
(1965, TRAFFIC JUDGE-STOLEN HOUR, BY MR. BUSHER)

Dam of 17 foals including:
Blush With Pride (1979 f. by Blushing Groom), winner of $536,807, Santa Susana S., Kentucky Oaks, Golden Harvest H., etc. Monroe (1977 f. by Sir Ivor) sent to Ireland, 3 wins. Minnie Hauk (1975 f. by Sir Ivor), Malinowski (1973 c. by Sir Ivor) champion 2-year-old colt in Ireland.

1983 COURTLY DEE
(1968, NEVER BEND-TULLE, BY WAR ADMIRAL)

Dam of 16 foals including:
Ali Oop (1974 c. by Al Hatab) 7 wins at 2 and 3, $174,020, Sapling S., Dragon S., 2nd Cowdin S., etc. Sire. Native Courier (1975 c. by Exclusive Native) 14 wins 2 to 7, $522,635, Laurel Turf Cup, Brighton Beach H., Bernard Baruch S. (twice), etc. Althea (1981 f. by Alydar) 1988 champion 2-year-old filly, 8 wins at 2 and 3, $1,275,255, Del Mar Debutante S., Arkansas Derby, Santa Susana S., etc. Also dam of stakes winner Princess Oola, Ketoh, Aihsah.

1984 HASTY QUEEN II
(1963, ONE COUNT-QUEEN HOPEFUL, BY ROMAN)

Dam of 16 foals, 12 winners including:
Hasty Flyer (1971 c. by Misty Flight) 15 wins 2 to 5, $293,663, Round Table H., 2nd Flamingo Stakes, etc. Sire. Hasty Tam (1975 c. by Tentam) 16 wins 2 to 6, $211,738, Ohio Open Championship H., Pegasus S., etc. Fit To Fight (1979 c. by Chieftain) 14 wins 2 to 5, $1,042,075, Jerome H., Stuyvesant H., Metropolitan H. etc. Also dam of stakes winners Hasty Cutie, Michael Navonod, Playful Queen.

1985 DUNCE CAP II
(1960, TOM FOOL-BRIGHT CORONET, BY BULL LEA)

Dam of 10 foals, 8 winners including:
Johnny Appleseed (1973 c. by Stage Door Johnny) 4 wins 2 to 3, $91,910, Louisiana Derby, 3rd Flamingo S., etc. Late Bloomer (1974 f. by Stage Door Johnny) 11 wins 2 to 5, $512,040, Beldame S., Sheepshead Bay H., Delaware H., etc. Late Act (1979 c. by Stage Door Johnny) 9 wins 3 to 7, $661,089, Louisiana Downs H. (twice), Cliff Hanger Stakes, etc.

1986 TOO BALD
(1964, BALD EAGLE-HIDDEN TALENT, BY DARK STAR)

Dam of 11 foals, 10 winners including:
Exceller (1973 c. by *Vaguely Noble) 15 wins 2 to 6, $1,125,772, Canadian International, Hollywood Gold Cup, Jockey Gold Cup, etc. Sire. Baldski (1974 c. by Nijinsky II) 7 wins 3 to 5, $103,214, Gold Coast H., 2nd Ak-Sar-Ben Omaha Gold H., etc. Sire. Capote (1984 c. by Seattle Slew) 10 wins 2 to 3, $714,470. 1986 champion 2-year-old colt, Breeders' Cup Juvenile, Norfolk S., etc.

1987 BANJA LUKA
(1968, DOUBLE JAY-LEGATO, BY DARK STAR)

Dam of 9 foals, 7 winners, 6 stakes winners including:
Ferdinand (1983 c. by Nijinsky II), Horse of the Year, 8 wins 2 to 4, $3,777,978, Kentucky Derby, Malibu S., Breeders' Cup Classic, Hollywood Gold Cup, 2nd Preakness, 3rd Belmont S., etc. Also dam of stakes winners: Jayston, Donna Inez, Ancient Art, Plinth, and Dancing.

1988 GRECIAN BANNER
(1974, HOIST THE FLAG-*DORINE, BY ARISTOPHANES)

Dam of 6 foals, 5 winners including:
Personal Flag (1983 c. by Private Account) 8 wins 3 to 5, $1,258,924, Widener H., Suburban H., etc. Personal Ensign (1984 f. by Private Account) 13 wins 2 to 4, $1,679,880, 1988 handicap female champion, Frizette S., Beldame S., Breeder's Cup Distaff, Whitney H., etc.

1989 RELAXING
(1976, BUCKPASSER-MARKING TIME, BY TO MARKET)

Dam of 6 foals, 4 winners, including:
Cadillacing (1984 f. by Alydar) 7 wins at 3 and 4, $268,137, Ballerina S., Distaff H., etc. Easy Goer (1986 c. by Alydar) 13 wins in 19 starts at 2 to 4. $4,634,370, champion 2-year-old colt, Belmont S., Woodward H., Champagne S., Wood Memorial, Whitney H., Cowdin S., etc.

LEADING SIRES

ACK ACK
(1966, BATTLE JOINED/FAST TURN, BY TURN-TO)

Stakes winner of 19 races, Horse of the Year, Champion Sprinter and Handicap horse. Sire of over 49 stakes winners including: Youth (champion grass horse at 3), Broad Brush ($2,656,793). Ack's Secret, etc.

ALYDAR
(1975, RAISE A NATIVE/SWEET TOOTH, BY ON-AND-ON)

Stakes winner of 14 races, $957,195. Sire of over 35 stakes winners including champions Alysheba (Horse of the Year, champion twice, world's leading money winner to 4, $6,679,242) Easy Goer (champion 2 year old, $3,859,650), Turkoman (Champion older horse, $2,146,924), Althea (champion 2-year-old filly, $1,275,255). Stakes winners include: Criminal Type ($2,337,090), Miss Oceana ($1,010,385), Clabber Girl ($1,006,261), etc.

BLENHEIM II
(1927, BLANDFORD/MALVA, BY CHARLES O'MALLEY)

Stakes winner of 5 in 10 starts. Sire of 60 stakes winners, including Whirlaway (Triple Crown, champion at 2 and 3, Horse of the Year, twice), Mahmoud (stakes winner, sire of 68 stakes winners), Mumtaz Begum (dam of Nasrullah, leading U.S. sire for 5 seasons), etc.

*BLUSHING GROOM
(1974, RED GOD-*RUNAWAY BRIDE, BY WILD RISK)

Champion in France and Europe. Sire of over 60 stakes winners including Blushing John ($908,030) Classic Tale (Horse of the Year in Belgium), Rainbow Quest (champion 3-year-old colt in Canada), Al Bahathri (champion 3-year-old in Ireland), etc.

BOLD RULER
(1954, *NASRULLAH MISS DISCO, BY DISCOVERY)

Stakes winner of 23 races, champion 3 year old colt, champion sprinter, leading sire of stakes winners 8 times, leading juvenile sire 5 times, leading sire 8 times, and sire of 82 stakes winners including 11 champions: Secretariat ($1,316,808, Horse of the Year at 2 and 3, Triple Crown, etc.) Gamely (champion 3-year-old filly), Wajima (champion 3-year-old colt), Successor (champion 2 year old), Bold Lad (champion 2 year old), Bold Bidder (champion handicap horse), Vitriolic (champion 2 year old), Queen Empress (champion 2-year-old filly), Lamb Chop (champion 3-year-old filly), Queen of the Stage (champion 2 year old), Bold Lad (champion 2 year old in England and Ireland, sire). Sire of sires.

BUCKPASSER
(1963, TOM FOOL-BUSANDA, BY WAR ADMIRAL)

Stakes winner of 25 races, $1,462,014, Horse of the Year, Champion 2 and 3 year old, Sire of 36 stakes winners including champions: Numbered Account (champion 2-year-old filly), Relaxing (champion handicap mare), La Prevoyante (champion 2-year-old filly), L'Enjoleur (Horse of the Year twice, leading freshman sire), Norcliffe (Canadian Horse of the Year, champion handicap horse, sire). Also leading broodmare sire.

BULL LEA
(1935, BULL DOG-ROSE LEAVES, BY BALLOT)

Stakes winner of 10 races. Leading sire 5 times. Sire of 27 stakes winners and nine champions including: Citation (32 wins, $1,085,760 Horse of the Year, champion at 2 and 3, Triple Crown), Armed (41 wins, Horse of the Year, champion handicap horse twice), Coaltown (23 wins, Horse of the Year, champion sprinter, champion handicap horse), Bewitch (champion filly at 2, champion handicap mare), Next Move (champion filly at 3) Two Lea (champion filly at 3, champion handicap mare) Twilight Tear (Horse of the Year, champion at 2 and 3, champion handicap mare), Durazna (champion filly at 2), etc.

COUNT FLEET
(1940, REIGH COUNT-QUICKLY, BY HASTE)

Stakes winner of 16 races, Triple Crown, champion 3-year-old, Horse of the Year. Leading sire, leading broodmare sire. Sire of 38 stakes winners including: Counterpoint (Horse of the Year), One Count (Horse of the Year), Kiss Me Kate (champion filly), etc.

DAMASCUS
(1964, SWORD DANCER-KERALA, BY *MY BABU)

Stakes winner of 21 races, $1,176,781, Horse of the Year at 3, champion 3-year-old, champion handicap horse. Sire of over 58 stakes winners including: Belted Earl (champion sprinter in Ireland), Lord Durham (champion 2 year old in Canada), Desert Wine ($1,618,043), Highland Blade ($998,888) Ogygian, Private Account, Honorable Miss, Eastern Echo, etc.

DANZIG
(1977, NORTHERN DANCER-PAS DE NOM, BY ADMIRAL'S VOYAGE)

Winner of 3 races in 3 starts. Sire of over 43 stakes winners including: Chief's Crown (champion 2-year-old, $2,191,168), Polonia (champion sprinter in France), Stephan's Odyssey ($1,255,328), Polish Navy ($1,118,076), Danzig Connection ($1,002,620), Dayjur, etc.

DEPUTY MINISTER
(1979, VICE REGENT-MINT COPY, BY BUNTY'S FLIGHT)

Horse of the Year in Canada, champion 2-year-old in U.S. and Canada. Sire of Open Mind (champion 2-year-old filly, $1,151,384), Go For Wand (champion at 2 and 3) King's Deputy, Deputy Shaw, Tejabo, Deputy Dancer, Eloquent Minister, etc.

DOUBLE JAY
(1944, BALLADIER-BROOMSHOT, BY WHISK BROOM II)

Champion 2-year-old. Sire of 45 stakes winners including: Doubledogdare (champion filly at 2 and 3), Spring Double, Tick Tock, Bagdad, Bupers, Sunrise Flight, Shirley Jones, etc.

DR. FAGER
(1964, ROUGH 'N TUMBLE-ASPIDISTRA, BY BETTER SELF)

Stakes winner of 18 races, $1,002,642, Horse of the Year. Sire of more than 35 stakes winners including: Dearly Precious (champion 2-year-old filly), L'Alezane (Canadian Horse of the Year), Practitioner, Tree of Knowledge, Lie Low, etc.

EXCLUSIVE NATIVE
(1965, RAISE A NATIVE-EXCLUSIVE, BY SHUT OUT)

Stakes winner. Leading sire twice, sire of more than 65 stakes winners including: Affirmed (Horse of the Year twice, champion colt at 2 and 3, champion handicap horse, Triple Crown, $2,393,818) Outstandingly ($1,412,206, champion 2-year-old filly), Genuine Risk (champion 3-year-old filly), Prodigo (champion 2-year-old colt in Puerto Rico. Sire), etc.

FAPPIANO
(1977, MR. PROSPECTOR-KILLALOE, BY DR. FAGER)

Stakes winner. Sire of more than 26 stakes winners including: Tasso (champion 2-year-old colt, $1,207,884), Cryptoclearance (12 wins to 5, $3,226,327), Tappiano ($1,305,522), Some Romance, Aptostar, Grand Canyon, Unbridled, etc.

GALLANT MAN
(1954, *MIGOLI-*MAJIDEH, BY *MAHMOUD)

Stakes winner, Co-leading sire of North American 1972 stakes winners. Sired 48 stakes winners including: Gallant Bloom (champion filly at 2 and 3, handicap mare), War Censor, Pattee Canyon, Gallant Romeo, Coraggioso, etc.

GRAUSTARK
(1963, *RIBOT-FLOWER BOWL, BY ALIBHAI)

Stakes winner of 7 races in 8 starts, 2nd once. Sire of over 48 stakes winners including: Key to the Mint (champion 3-year-old colt), Tempest Queen (champion 3-year-old filly), Caracolero (champion 3-year-old colt in France) Stakes winners include: Proud Truth ($2,198,895), Gregorian, Ruritania, Distant Land, etc.

HAIL TO REASON
(1958, *TURN-TO-NOTHIRDCHANCE, BY BLUE SWORDS)

Stakes winner of 9 races. Leading sire and leading juvenile sire in 1970. Sire of champions: Straight Deal (champion handicap horse), Personality (Horse of the Year), Trillion (champion older mare in France, champion grass mare in U.S.), Roberto (champion 2-year-old in Ireland), Regal Gleam (champion 2-year-old filly), Hippodamia (champion 2-year-old filly in France). Stakes winners include: Stop The Music, Limit To Reason, Cum Laude Laurie, Hail To All, Mr. Leader, Proud Clarion, Halo, etc.

HALO
(1969, HAIL TO REASON-COSMAH, BY COSMIC BOMB)

Stakes winner. Sire of more than 40 stakes winners including champions: Sunny's Halo (champion 2-year-old colt in Canada, $1,247,791), Glorious Song (champion mare, Canadian Horse of the Year, $1,004,534), Devil's Bag (champion 2-year-old colt), Sunday Silence (champion 3-year-old colt, Horse of the Year, $1,418,530), Tilt My Halo, Rainbow Connection, etc.

*HERBAGER
(1958, VANDALE-FLAGETTE, BY ESCAMILLO)

Stakes winner in 6 of 8 starts, champion 3-year-old colt in France. Co-leading sire of stakes winners 1971, among leading sires in France and the U.S. Sire of 62 stakes winners including: Our Mims (champion 3-year-old filly), *Grey Dawn II (champion at 2), Appiani (champion in Italy at 3), Tiller, Big Spruce, etc.

HIS MAJESTY
(1968, *RIBOT-FLOWER BOWL, BY ALIBHAI)

Stakes winner. Sire of over 31 stakes winners including: Pleasant Colony (champion 3-year-old colt), Asaltante (champion handicap colt in Mexico), Panjandrum (champion 2-year-old colt in Italy). Stakes winners include: Majesty's Prince (12 wins 2 to 5, $2,030,451), Mehmet, Andover Way, Cormorant, Frosty The Snowman, Batonnier, Pleasant Tap, etc.

HOIST THE FLAG
(1968, TOM ROLFE-WAVY NAVY, BY WAR ADMIRAL)

Stakes winner, champion 2-year-old colt. Sire of 51 stakes winners including: Sensational (champion 2-year-old filly), Alleged (9 wins in 10 starts, Horse of the Year twice in Europe, champion 3-year-old colt in France and England), True Colors, Flying Above, Fifth Marine, Stalwart, Linkage, Flying Partner, Thirty Flags, etc.

IN REALITY
(1964, INTENTIONALLY-MY DEAR GIRL, BY ROUGH 'N TUMBLE)

Stakes winner. Sire of 71 stakes winners including champions: Smile ($1,664,027, champion sprinter), Desert Vixen (champion at 3 and 4), Known Fact (champion in England). Stakes winners include: Ring Of Light, Proper Reality, Star Choice, Believe It, Relaunch, etc.

INTENTIONALLY
(1956, INTENT-MY RECIPE, BY DISCOVERY)

Stakes winner of 18 races, champion sprinter. Sire of 20 stakes winners including: Ta Wee (champion sprinter), In Reality, Red Reality, Tentam, Hey Rube, etc.

MAN O'WAR
(1917, FAIR PLAY-MAHUBAH, BY ROCK SAND)

Stakes winner of 20 races from 21 starts. Champion at 2 and 3 and Horse of the Year. Leading sire of 1926. Sire of 64 stakes winners including: War Admiral (1937 Triple Crown winner, champion 3-year-old colt and Horse of the Year, leading sire of 1945), War Relic (winner of 9 races, sire of 14 stakes winners including Relic and Intent), etc.

MR. PROSPECTOR
(1970, RAISE A NATIVE-GOLD DIGGER, BY NASHUA)

Stakes winner. Leading sire twice, sire of more than 95 stakes winners including: Conquistador Cielo (champion 3-year-old colt, Horse of the Year), Gulch ($3,095,521, champion sprinter), Forty Niner ($2,726,000, champion 2-year-old colt), It's In The Air (Horse of the Year in Canada), Ravinella (champion at 2 and 3 in England and France), Eillo (champion sprinter), Tersa (champion 2-year-old filly in France), Gold Beauty (champion sprinter), Woodman (champion 2-year-old colt in Ireland). Stakes winners Seeking The Gold ($2,307,000), Tank Prospect ($1,355,645), Homebuilder ($1,138,868), Fappiano, etc.

NASHUA
(1952, *NASRULLAH-SEGULA, BY JOHNSTOWN)

Stakes winner of 22 races, $1,288,565, champion at 2 and 3, Horse of the Year at 3. Sire of 77 stakes winners, including: Shuvee (champion handicap mare at 4 and 5, 16 wins 2 to 5), Producer. Diplomat Way (14 wins 2 to 4), Fairway Flyer, Marshua (champion 3-year-old filly in France), etc.

*NASRULLAH
(1935, NEARCO-MUMTAZ BEGUM, BY BLENHEIM II)

Stakes winner. Leading sire in England and leading U.S. sire five times. Sire of 101 stakes winners including: Noor (champion handicap male), Nashua (Horse of the Year), Bold Ruler (Horse of the Year), Bald Eagle (champion handicap male), Jaipur (champion 3-year-old colt), Never Bend (champion 2-year-old colt). Also One-Eyed King, Red God, Fleet Nasrullah, Nadir, etc.

NATIVE DANCER
(1950, POLYNESIAN-GEISHA, BY DISCOVERY)

Classic winner of 21 races in 22 starts, champion at 2 and 3, champion older horse, Horse of the Year twice. Sire of 45 stakes winners including: Raise A Native (undefeated stakes winner of 4 races, champion 2-year-old colt, among leading sires), Hula Dancer (champion 2-year-old filly in France), etc.

NEARCO
(1935, PHAROS-NOGARA, BY HAVRESAC II)

Stakes winner of 14 races in 14 starts. Leading sire in England 3 times, sire of 109 stakes winners including: *Nasrullah (leading sire in England, U.S. leading sire 5 times, sire of 101 stakes winners), Royal Charger (stakes winner in England, leading sire in England and U.S., sire of 58 stakes winners), Nearctic (stakes winner of 21 races, Canadian Horse of the Year at 4, among the leading sires in U.S. and France, sire of 49 stakes winners including champions Northern Dancer and Icecapade), etc.

NEARCTIC
(1954, NEARCO-*LADY ANGELA, BY HYPERION)

Stakes winner of 21 races in 47 starts, Canadian Horse of the Year at 4, Leading sire of North American stakes winners in 1971, leading juvenile sire in France in 1973. Sire of 49 stakes winners including: Northern Dancer (champion 3-year-old colt, Canadian Horse of the Year, 14 wins in 18 starts at 2

149

and 3), Bye And Near (champion handicap horse in Canada), Not Too Shy (champion 3-year-old filly and handicap mare in Canada), Cool Reception (champion 2-year-old colt in Canada), Ice Water (Champion handicap mare in Canada), Rouletabille (champion 3-year-old colt in Canada), Ice-capade, North Sea, Briartic, etc.

NEVER BEND
(1960, *NASRULLAH-LALUN, BY *DJEDDAH)

Stakes winner, champion 2-year-old colt. Leading sire in England in 1971, leading freshman sire in U.S. in 1967. Sire of over 60 stakes winners including: Mill Reef (European Horse of the Year at 3, champion 3-year-old colt in Europe, champion older male in Europe, leading sire in England), J. O. Tobin (champion 2-year-old colt in England, champion sprinter in U.S.), Gelinotte (17 wins to 3, Horse of the Year, in Venezuela, champion filly at 2 and 3), Riverman (5 wins in 8 starts in France, leading sire), Torsion, etc.

NIJINSKY II
(1967, NORTHERN DANCER-FLAMING PAGE, BY BULL PAGE)

Champion 2-year-old colt in England and Ireland, Horse of the Year and champion at 3 in England; winner English Triple Crown. Sire of more than 115 stakes winners, 9 champions including: Ferdinand ($3,777,978,

Horse of the Year, champion older male), De La Rose (champion grass female), Ile De Bourbon (champion 3-year-old colt in England), Shahrastani (champion 3-year-old colt in Ireland), Golden Fleece (champion 3-year-old colt in England and Ireland), Caerleon (champion 3-year-old colt in France), Shadeed (champion 3-year-old colt in England), Princesse Lida (champion 2-year-old filly in France), Cherry Hinton (champion 2-year-old filly in England), Kings Lake (champion 3-year-old colt in England and France), Solford (champion 3-year-old colt in Ireland), etc.

NORTHERN DANCER
(1961, NEARCTIC-NATALMA, BY NATIVE DANCER)

Champion 3-year-old in North America (Kentucky Derby). Sire of more than 105 stakes winners, 26 champions including: Nijinsky II (champion 2-year-old colt in England and Ireland, Horse of the Year and champion at 3 in England), The Minstrel (Horse of the Year in England, sire), Northernette (Canadian champion filly at 2 and 3), Try My Best (champion 2-year-old colt in England and Ireland), Fanfreluche (Canadian champion 3-year-old filly and Horse of the Year), Nureyev (champion 3-year-old colt in France, sire), El Gran Senor, Storm Bird, Danzig, Lyphard, Topsider, etc. Sire of sires.

NUREYEV
(1977, NORTHERN DANCER-SPECIAL, BY *FORLI)

Champion miler in France. Leading sire in France, sire of more than 40 stakes winners including: Theatrical (champion grass horse, champion older male in Ireland, $2,946,853), Miesque (champion grass female twice, champion 2-year-old filly in France, champion 3-year-old filly in England and France, champion older female in France), Sonic Lady (champion 3-year-old filly in France, England, and Ireland, champion older female in England), Soviet Star (champion 3-year-old colt in France), Stately Don (champion 3-year-old colt in Ireland), etc.

PRINCE JOHN
(1953, *PRINCEQUILLO-NOT AFRAID, BY COUNT FLEET)

Stakes winner, leading juvenile sire in 1969. Sire of 53 stakes winners including: Typecast (21 wins, 3 to 6, champion handicap mare), Silent Screen (champion 2-year-old colt), Stage Door Johnny (Champion 3-year-old colt), Protagonist (champion 2-year-old colt), etc.

*PRINCEQUILLO
(1940, PRINCE ROSE-*COSQUILLA, BY PAPYRUS)

Stakes winner of 12 races, 2 to 4. Leading sire twice in U.S. and once in Ireland, sire of 65 stakes winners, 6 champions including;

Round Table (Horse of the Year, champion handicap horse twice, champion grass horse 3 times, 43 wins, 2 to 5, $1,749,869), Dedicate (Horse of the Year, champion handicap horse), Hill Prince (Horse of the Year, champion at 2 and 3, champion handicap horse, sire), Quill (champion 2-year-old filly), Misty Morn (champion 3-year-old filly, champion handicap mare), Prince Simon (champion 3-year-old colt), etc.

PRIVATE ACCOUNT
(1976, DAMASCUS-NUMBERED ACCOUNT, BY BUCKPASSER)

Stakes winner. Sire of more than 15 stakes winners including: Personal Ensign (undefeated, $1,679,880, champion older female), Personal Flag ($1,258,924), Private Terms, ($1,242,947), Classy Cathy, Miserden, Chimes of Freedom, Silent Account, etc.

RAISE A NATIVE
(1961, NATIVE DANCER-RAISE YOU, BY CASE ACE)

Stakes winner, champion 2-year-old colt, Leading juvenile sire. Sire of over 45 stakes winners including: Crowned Prince (champion 2-year-old colt), Laomedonte (champion 3-year-old colt), Alydar, Majestic Prince, Native Royalty, Raisela, Raise a Man, Mr. Prospector, Exclusive Native, etc.

RAJA BABA
(1968, BOLD RULER-MISSY BABA, BY MY BABU)

Stakes winner, leading sire in North America in 1980, leading sire of 2-year-olds in 1976 and 1980. Sire of over 58 stakes winners including: Sacahuista (champion 3-year-old filly) Gran Zar (Horse of the Year in Mexico), Summer Mood (champion sprinter in Canada), Well Decorated, Sweet Revenge, etc.

RELAUNCH
(1976, IN REALITY-FOGGY NOTE, BY THE AXE II)

Stakes winner. Sire of more than 25 stakes winners including: Relasure (champion older mare in Italy), Skywalker ($2,226,750), Waquoit ($2,225,360), Calestoga, Overage, Carload, etc.

*RIBOT
(1952, TENERANI-ROMANELLA, BY EL GRECO)

Stakes winner of 16 races from 16 starts. Champion 2-year-old colt, Horse of the Year in Europe at 3 and 4. Leading sire three times in England, among the leading sires in France and U.S. Sire of 66 stakes winners including: Tom Rolfe (16 wins 2 to 4, champion 3-year-old colt, leading freshman sire, among the leading sires), Arts and Letters (Horse of the Year, champion 3-year-old colt, among the leading sires), Ribocco (champion at 3 in Ireland), Ragusa (champion at 3 in Ireland), *Prince Royal II (champion 3-year-old colt in France), Molvedo (champion at 2 and 3), Ribofilio (champion miler in England), Romulus (champion miler in England), Alice Frey (champion 3-year-old filly). Stakes winners include Graustark (7 wins in 8 starts, among the leading sires), etc.

ROBERTO
(1969, HAIL TO REASON-BRAMALEA, BY NASHUA)

Champion 2-year-old colt in Ireland, champion 3-year-old colt in England. Among the leading sires in England and U.S. Sire of over 65 stakes winners including: Sunshine Forever ($2,073,800, champion grass horse), Driving Home (champion older horse in Canada), Legarto (champion 2-year-old filly in Canada), Sookera (champion 2-year-old filly in Ireland), Critique (champion 2-year-old colt in France), Lear Fan, Hey Babe, etc.

ROUND TABLE
(1954, *PRINCEQUILLO-KNIGHT'S DAUGHTER, BY SIR COSMO)

Stakes winner $1,749,869, champion handicap horse twice, Horse of the Year, champion grass horse three times, stakes winner of 43 races. Leading sire in 1972, leading sire of stakes winners in 1973 and 74, sire of 82 stakes winners including: Baldric (champion miler in England), Apalachee (champion 2-year-old colt in England and Ireland), Flirting Around (champion older horse in England), Targowice (champion 2-year-old colt in France), He's a Smoothie (Horse of the Year in Canada, champion handicap horse twice in Canada), Drumtop, Royal Glint, ($1,004,816), etc.

ROYAL CHARGER
(1942, NEARCO-SUN PRINCESS, BY SOLARIO)

Stakes winner of 6 races in England, among leading sires in England and U.S. Sire of 58 stakes winners including: Mongo (champion grass horse sire), Royal Native (champion filly at 3, champion mare), Idun (champion at 2 and 3), *Royal Serenade (champion sprinter in England, among leading juvenile sires), Turn-To, etc.

SEATTLE SLEW
(1974, BOLD REASONING-MY CHARMER, BY POKER)

Champion at 2 and 3, Horse of the Year, winner of the Triple Crown, $1,208,726. Leading sire, sire of more than 30 stakes winners, including: Slew o'Gold ($3,533,534, champion 3-year-old colt and older horse), Swale ($1,583,660, champion 3-year-old colt), Capote (champion 2-year-old colt at 2), Landaluce (champion 2-year-old filly at 2), Slew City Slew, ($1,029,400), Tsunami Slew, Slewpy, etc.

SECRETARIAT
(1970, BOLD RULER-SOMETHINGROYAL, BY *PRINCEQUILLO)

Horse of the Year at 2 and 3, champion colt at 2 and 3, champion grass horse at 3, winner of Triple Crown, $1,316,808. Sire of over 40 stakes winners including: Lady's Secret (Horse of the Year, champion older mare, world's leading money-winning mare, 25 wins, $3,021,325), Risen Star (champion 3-year-old colt, 8 wins to 3, $2,029,845), Medaille d'Or (champion 2-year-old colt in Canada), Pancho Villa, General Assembly, Terlingua, Weekend Surprise, Clever Secret, etc.

SIR IVOR
(1965, SIR GAYLORD-ATTICA, BY MR. TROUBLE)

Stakes winner in England, Ireland, France, and North America. Champion 2-year-old colt in Ireland, champion 3-year-old colt and Horse of the Year in England. Sire of: Bates Motel (champion handicap horse), Ivor's Image (champion filly in Italy at 2 and 3), Ivanjica (champion 3-year-old filly and handicap mare in France), Malinowski (champion 2-year-old colt in Ireland, sire) Cloonlara (champion 2-year-old filly in Ireland), Godetia (champion 3-year-old filly in Ireland) St. Hilarion (champion 3-year-old colt in Italy), etc.

STAGE DOOR JOHNNY
(1965, PRINCE JOHN-PEROXIDE BLONDE, BY BALLYMOSS)

Stakes winner. Champion 3-year-old colt. Sire of over 46 stakes winners including: Johnny D. (champion grass horse), Late Bloomer (champion handicap mare) Open Call, Johnny's Image, Class Play, etc .

T.V. LARK
(1957, *INDIAN HEMP-MISS LARKSFLY, BY HEELFLY)

Stakes winner of 19 races, $902,194, champion grass horse. Leading sire in 1974. Leading sire and juvenile sire of 53 stakes winners including: Buffalo Lark, Quack, Golden Don, T. V. Vixen, T. V. Commercial, Romeo, etc.

TOM FOOL
(1949, MENOW-GAGA, BY *BULL DOG)

Stakes winner of 21 races, champion 2-year-old, champion handicap horse, sprinter, Horse of the Year at 4 (undefeated in 10 starts). Among the leading sires in U.S. and England. Leading broodmare sire in England, leading juvenile sire. Sire of more than 36 stakes winners, including: Buckpasser ($1,462,014, Horse of the Year, champion 2-year-old colt and handicap horse Sire), Tim Tam (champion 3-year-old colt), Tompion, Dunce, Cyrano, etc.

TOM ROLFE
(1962, *RIBOT-POCAHONTAS, BY ROMAN)

Stakes winner of 16 races, champion 3-year-old colt. Sire of over 46 stakes winners including: Bowl Game (champion grass horse), Run the Gantlet (champion grass horse), Hoist the Flag (champion 2-year-old colt) Droll Role (champion grass horse in Canada), Alez Milord (champion 3-year-old colt in Germany), etc. Leading broodmare sire.

TURN-TO
(1951, *ROYAL CHARGER-*SOURCE SUSRESS, BY ADMIRAL DRAKE)

Stakes winner of 6 of 8 starts. Among the leading sires of stakes winners. Sire of over 26 stakes winners including: First Landing (champion 2-year-old colt), Best Turn (among the leading sires), Nibelungo (champion 3-year-old colt in Mexico), Sir Gaylord, Cyane, etc.

*VAGUELY NOBLE
(1965, VIENNA-NOBLE LASIE, BY NEARCO)

European Horse of the Year, leading sire twice in England, sire of more than 60 stakes winners, including: Dahlia (English Horse of the Year twice, champion 5 times), Estrapade (champion older mare in France, champion turf mare in North America, $1,924,588), Lemhi Gold ($1,129,585, champion older horse in North America, Sire), El Cuite (champion 3-year-old colt in Italy and France), Noble Decree (champion colt at 2 in England), Mississipian (champion at 2 or 3 colt in France, sire), Gay Mecene (champion older male in France), Empery (champion 3-year-colt in England), Friendswood (champion 3-year-old filly in Italy), Exceller ($1,662,003), etc.

VICE REGENT
(1967, NORTHERN DANCER-VICTORIA REGINA, BY MENETRIER)

Sire of over 59 stakes winners including: Deputy Minister (champion 2-year-old colt, Horse of the Year and champion 2-year-old colt in Canada), Bessarabian (champion older mare in Canada), Fraud Squad (champion sprinter in Canada), Christy's Mount (champion older mare and handicap mare in Canada), Bounding Away (champion grass horse in Canada, Deceit Dancer (champion 2-year-old filly in Canada), Ruling Angel (Horse of the Year in Canada, champion 2-year-old filly in Canada), etc.

DESIGN BY J.-C. SUARÈS

COMPOSED IN GARAMOND STEMPEL BY TRUFONT TYPOGRAPHERS, HICKSVILLE, NY

PRINTED AND BOUND BY TIEN WAH PRESS (PTE.) LTD., SINGAPORE